I0755001

To

From

Date

THE 5-MINUTE Teen Girl DEVOTIONAL

Building Resilience and Hope

The 5-Minute Teen Girl Devotional: Building Resilience and Hope

First Edition, May 2025

Published by:

21154 Highway 16 East
Siloam Springs, AR 72761
dayspring.com

Written By: Kristin Cortner
Cover Design by: Becca Barnett

Printed in China
Prime: U3371
ISBN: 979-8-88603-030-3

Contents

Section 3: A Flood of Emotions

Section 4: Relational Creations

Section 5: From Sprout to Seedling

Introduction

These teenage years are such an amazing time in your life. You're growing into the woman you'll become. You're leaving behind those years of childhood. You're experiencing new emotions. New challenges. New experiences. There is no season of life quite like the teenage years. It's a time of fluctuating feelings and roller-coaster relationships. These years will bring difficulties and big wins all at the same time. My friend, this is just the beginning of what God has in store for you!

We'll have lots of fun through this devotional. We'll explore characters from the Bible, chat about this sticky "in-between" season, and learn from my own teenage misadventures. We'll talk about the hard things and laugh about the funny issues we all face. I hope you enjoy this journey. If you only take one thing away from this devotional book, let it be this: You are a beautiful daughter of God. He crafted you with such care. He put you together in a precise way for an important reason. There is no one else like you. You're amazing. You're remarkable. You're a true world-changer. A person with a purpose. Ready to truly believe that? Right now is a great time to start.

Kristen Cortner

SECTION 1

Vital Truths

"You will experience for yourselves the truth, and the truth will free you."

JOHN 8:31–32 THE MESSAGE

Core Identity

My old self has been crucified with Christ.
It is no longer I who live, but Christ lives in me.
So I live in this earthly body by trusting in the Son of God,
who loved me and gave Himself for me.

GALATIANS 2:20 NLT

Who are you?

Take a moment to think on that question. If you're sitting close to a notepad and pen, jot down a few answers. Perhaps you have "daughter" or "cheerleader" or "academic" on your list. Maybe you play an instrument or sing in the choir. Maybe you're an outstanding track star or someone who is great at art. These are all the components of your life that make you who you are. You are unique. You are special. There is no one else quite like you. When we're teenagers, we spend a lot of time deciding what that list will look like. Even if we don't consciously think about it all the time, that question is always there in the background: *Who am I?*

You're in a season of self-discovery. You're growing up. Your body is developing into your adult body. Your personality is changing. Your sense of humor is adjusting. Everything is moving forward in leaps and bounds. It can feel so easy to feel like life is running ahead without you. It's okay if you don't have much to write down to answer that question. If that question freaked you out and made you nervous, you're not alone. It makes *everyone* nervous. And I'll let you in on a big secret: adults don't have the answers to it either.

Take a marker and scratch out the first word in the question, and replace "who" with "whose."

Whose are you?

Now, this is a question we can all answer. It takes no self-discovery. No nervous worrying. No wishing or feeling like we aren't enough. You are His. You are God's beloved daughter. A gift that He carefully crafted. You are adored by your Father in heaven, and He created you for a purpose. Everything that makes you who you are was carefully chosen and selected by God. You are here for a reason. And you are vitally important.

Dear Jesus, thank You for creating me to be me. Thank You for loving me. I am Your daughter, and I am never alone. Walk with me today. Amen.

Completed

"For this is how God loved the world:
He gave His one and only Son, so that everyone
who believes in Him will not perish but have eternal life."

JOHN 3:16 NLT

There are some very important, *vital* pieces of truth that each of us needs to know. In a world where "truth" changes based on people's whims, we've lost sight of what absolute truth is. Here's one extremely important truth for you to hold close to your heart today: Jesus completed His work.

Jesus willingly went to the cross and died a brutal death on our behalf. Humankind's relationship to God the Father had been severed by our own bad choices. But our loving God so desperately wanted to fix the rift that He sent His own Son, Jesus Christ, to earth to become the sacrifice needed to bridge the gap that our sins had created.

Read today's verse again. You might have memorized it in children's Sunday school. You might have seen it painted on billboards or on a bumper sticker. But let the core truth of it sink into your heart today. God loves you. He wants to have a friendship and lifelong relationship with you, His daughter.

Without Jesus, we are separated from God because of all the wrong choices we make, which the Bible calls *sin*. We are like little children who run into a dark room and can't find our way out. God sent Jesus to be our light, and He is waiting for each of us with an outstretched hand, ready to lead us out of the darkness and into a fulfilling life here on earth and into eternal life in heaven after we die.

The work that Jesus did on the cross was a huge moment in history. His last word was *tetelestai,* which in Greek means, "it is finished." The work is done. The bridge between us and God was remade. And now we never, ever have to walk in this world alone. This is a truth that changes lives. Reshapes hearts. Puts us on a new path. Is it a truth that you wholeheartedly believe?

Dear Jesus, thank You for going to the cross willingly for me. Thank You for defeating sin and death and completing the work of redemption. I love You. Amen.

YOUR MOVE:

What does this vital truth mean to you? Grab a piece of paper and pen and write down your thoughts about the completed work of Jesus.

Elusive Confidence

Don't be obsessed with getting more material things.
Be relaxed with what you have. Since God assured us,
"I'll never let you down, never walk off and leave you,"
we can boldly quote, "God is there, ready to help;
I'm fearless no matter what. Who or what can get to me?"

HEBREWS 13:5-6 THE MESSAGE

Don't we all wish we could feel more confident in ourselves? Self-doubt follows us wherever we go, ready to tap us on the shoulder at a moment's notice and remind us that we're not quite good enough. Let me reveal a well-kept secret: confidence doesn't come with age. That's right. Adult women struggle with confidence each and every day. As you grow through your teenage years, confidence might become harder and harder to find. Gone are the innocent days of being a kid, when no one cared about how you looked, what clothes you wore, or where you were from. Now you care how people perceive you, and that is something that isn't going to go away with graduation.

Confidence is slippery, isn't it? Maybe you can fake it until you make it and force everyone to believe you have it together. But most of us can't fake confidence.

It's so hard to feel like we're good enough when everything in our world is shouting at us that we aren't. I had braces for five years during my junior high and high school years. I didn't get them off until right before my senior year. I was so embarrassed about my braces. I never wanted to smile. I cried in the bathroom when I knew picture day was coming up. The fear of what people whispered about me consumed me. Now I realize they probably didn't care in the least that I had braces. They were too consumed with their own self-doubts. But it really mattered to me.

I wish I could just go back in time and give that fifteen-year-old girl a hug. It's okay to have self-doubt. We all have it. But the truth is that confidence comes when we embrace who we are. In today's verse, the writer of Hebrews says, "I'm fearless no matter what" because "God is there, ready to help." Fearlessness and confidence are good buddies. Love who you are. You are so incredibly special.

Dear Lord, thank You for making me just the way I am.
Please help me learn how to love all my rough edges.
True confidence comes from You. Amen.

The Comparison Game

Oh, don't worry; we wouldn't dare say that we are as wonderful as these other men who tell you how important they are! But they are only comparing themselves with each other, using themselves as the standard of measurement. How ignorant!

II CORINTHIANS 10:12 NLT

Competition can be really fun. Sitting in the stands at a football game while you cheer for your favorite team is awesome. Playing your instrument at a marching band contest or competing in a tournament fills you with adrenaline, drive, and discipline. God made us to feel a level of competition because it is a motivator to be the best we can be. Winning is sweet.

But the comparison game we play with each other is a game we cannot win. Let me say it in a different way. No one *ever* wins when we play the comparison game. Can you guess why? It's pretty simple. You can't be anyone other than yourself. So when you compare your clothes, your skin, your body type, your voice, or anything else, with someone else, there's no victory in it. Even if you go online or to the store that very day and buy the exact same outfit as her, you're still you, and there is always something else to compare. The comparison game is an exhausting, never-ending battle to fit in and stay afloat of ever-changing trends. The moment we buy the newest shoe brand or get the hairstyle that everyone else has, the trend has changed, and we are already out of style.

Don't play the comparison game. It's not a game that God created us to play. We are meant to encourage one another. Don't try to be anyone that you're not. Even the prettiest, most popular girl at school wishes she could change something about herself. Embrace who you are and who God made you to be. Chances are, someone has looked at you and compared themselves to what you have. Be the person who lifts others up and helps people feel comfortable in their own bodies. You are an amazing person, and God wants you to be exactly who you are. No one else.

Lord, thank You for making me just the way that I am. I pray that I can be someone who uplifts other people. Show me who to encourage today. Amen.

YOUR MOVE:

Find two people to compliment today.

The Search for Meaning

When He saw the crowds, He had compassion on them because they were confused and helpless, like sheep without a shepherd. He said to His disciples, "The harvest is great, but the workers are few. So pray to the Lord who is in charge of the harvest; ask Him to send more workers into His fields."

MATTHEW 9:36–38 NLT

Let's say that you're sitting on your couch and you grab the remote to find a new show to watch. You remember your friend mentioning a show recently, but you can't remember what it was called. Was it on Netflix? Hulu? You remember the general plot and that it was a trending show for teens. What do you do? If you have a smartphone, you're probably already pulling it out and opening up your Google app. One short query later, and ta-da, there's your friend's new favorite TV show, now streaming on Netflix.

Google's company mission statement is "to organize the world's information and make it universally accessible and useful."[1] Essentially, Google capitalized on an essential human truth many years ago and has

1 https://www.google.com/search/howsearchworks/our-approach/

made billions of dollars. And that vital truth is: *everybody is searching for something.*

We are all on a journey of discovery, and the season of life you're in right now is a big one. You're discovering who you are, who you're going to be, and what this big world is really like. You're asking new questions, wondering about hard topics, and potentially freaking out about the future on a daily basis. The greatest search query you'll ever ponder is: *What does my life mean?*

Jesus spent years of His life traveling around the countryside of Israel and teaching people about God's love. He had great compassion on all of the people He saw because He understood that they were all confused and helpless. They were like a huge flock of sheep, milling about in absolute chaos. Lost.

Just like Jesus had compassion on the crowds of people in His day, He has compassion on you. You aren't lost. Your life does have special meaning. You're here for a purpose, and that purpose is fulfilled when you learn to love God and follow Jesus. The journey has just begun.

Dear Jesus, thank You for answering my search for meaning. Thank You for giving me a reason to live each and every day. Help me to lead my lost friends to You. Amen.

Crafted by the Potter

And yet, O Lord, You are our Father.
We are the clay, and You are the potter.
We all are formed by Your hand.

ISAIAH 64:8 NLT

If you've never witnessed a master potter at the pottery wheel, you should. Artisans have been spinning clay into art for thousands of years. It takes incredible skill to maintain the steady speed of the wheel while the potter slowly molds the mound of gray clay into something more, something with intention behind it. Then, once the vase is formed, they begin the beautification process, using paints and textures to make the art piece special and unique.

We all started out as globs of clay, and God breathed life into us when we were growing in our mother's womb. None of us had shape or form until the Lord started to create us just the way we are. God is an artist. Take a look around the world we live in. From majestic mountain ranges to rushing waterfalls to the dunes of the desert, we live in a beautiful place. God put just as much thought and intention into creating you as He did creating this entire planet. Your body is made of up millions of neurons and atoms and cells, all massing together to form your muscles, your organs, your bones. You.

You are a miracle, and God designed you with love in His heart with a purpose for your life.

Everyone wishes they could change something about themselves. For me, I've always disliked my nose and the fact that one of my eyes is slightly smaller than the other. That probably seems silly to you, but I spent countless minutes of my teenage years trying to find ways to hide these small "imperfections."

We live in a world where perfection is impossible, and yet we still try so hard to mold ourselves into something new and different. God crafted each and every hair on your head, each freckle on your face, the color of your skin, everything. He designed you like the most beautiful piece of pottery in the world. He molded you so carefully into who you are. You are amazing. You are so beautiful. You are such a gift.

God, thank You for creating me with so much care. Thank You for loving me so much. I am so glad that You are my Father, and that I get to be Your creation. Amen.

Never Alone

Be strong. Take courage. Don't be intimidated.
Don't give them a second thought because God,
your God, is striding ahead of you. He's right there with you.
He won't let you down; He won't leave you.

DEUTERONOMY 31:6 THE MESSAGE

At the end of the book of Deuteronomy, the Israelites are in a tough spot. They have escaped from slavery in Egypt, crossed the Red Sea, wandered around the desert for forty years, and have now arrived at the Promised Land, the land that God had granted them to settle. They were worn out by this point, but they had always had Moses to lead them. Moses had been God's messenger who brought them out of Egypt. He had given them the Ten Commandments and the Law. He had been their trusted leader. And now he was about to die.

The Israelites felt totally and completely alone and abandoned as they watched their leader reach the end of his life. Moses gathered the people together and gave them this direction: "Be strong. Take courage . . . your God is striding ahead of you. He's right there with you" (Deuteronomy 31:6). Moses wanted to remind his people that even though he was departing, they weren't alone. God was with them.

You might be in a season of intense loneliness. Perhaps you feel like there is no one to turn to. Maybe you feel abandoned by people you trusted. Maybe you feel like you're alone in the desert with no one to lead you home. It's okay to feel lonely sometimes. But the vital truth here is that you are *never* alone. Even if you flew to a deserted island with no other people around, you still would not be alone. How? God is with you. If you have given your life to God, then His Holy Spirit dwells within you, which means that wherever you go, whatever you do, God will be right there, ready to answer your call for help and to provide comfort when you need Him most. There have been many times in my life when I've begged the Lord to help me, and He has always been there. You're never alone. You have the God of the universe right there with you today, tomorrow, and always.

Lord, thank You for walking with me when I feel alone. Thank You for being there for each and every one of us. I'm so glad that I never have to feel alone. Amen.

100%

But God is so rich in mercy, and He loved us so much,
that even though we were dead because of our sins,
He gave us life when He raised Christ from the dead.
(It is only by God's grace that you have been saved!)

EPHESIANS 2:4–5 NLT

Everyone loves to get an A+ on a homework assignment or test. They are rare, but when it happens, it's the best feeling because we have achieved a perfect score. 100%. We didn't miss a beat. It's so rare that we ever see 100% in life. No politician wins 100% of the votes. No home project is ever 100% complete. And no one, no matter how much we grow in life, is ever 100% perfect. There is no absolute in life except when it comes to Truth with a capital *T*. We live in a world of "choose your own truth." Everyone makes up their own truths and expects everyone else to respect their realities. Truth has become so lost in this world that people will believe anything others say if it's said with conviction and some statistics to boot.

Never lose sight of real, absolute Truth. And that Truth is that God loves you. God is real, and He has a plan for this messed up world. He doesn't want you to walk alone, and He cares for you 100%. Totally. Completely. Not 99%. Not 99.9%. It's absolute. And nothing we say or do will change God's love for His children. Let that sink in today. As you go about your daily life, as you interact with other students, your siblings, your parents, think about that. We could never give 100% of ourselves because we aren't perfect. But Jesus did. He gave us His 100%. He sacrificed Himself on the cross for our wrongs, and He rose from the dead to conquer sin once and for all. We can be 100% redeemed because of His 100% perfection. Come on, girl. That's something to smile about! You're 100% loved. 100% redeemed. 100% made new because of Jesus. Don't forget that absolute Truth when you grab your backpack and head out the door. You're already winning the day.

Jesus, thank You for giving your 100%
so I can be 100% loved. I am so grateful to You for
Your sacrifice so I can experience redemption. Amen.

YOUR MOVE:

Read the entire chapter of Ephesians 2 and write down a few 100% truths that you see.

Tug-of-War

Therefore, put on every piece of God's armor so you will be able to resist the enemy in the time of evil. Then after the battle you will still be standing firm.

EPHESIANS 6:13 NLT

Did you know that tug-of-war used to be an Olympic sport? The United States won gold in tug-of-war in 1904. If you've never played tug-of-war, it involves two teams. Both teams line up on either end of a rope. The teams pull the rope in their direction, hoping to eventually tug the rope until the flag in the middle makes it over a certain spot. It takes a lot of strength and perseverance to play tug-of-war.

We live in a daily game of tug-of-war. If you're a Christian, there is an opposing team constantly trying to drag you to their side, and that is the side of the devil, the enemy of all Christians. He often tempts Christians to stumble and fall. A fallen player is much easier to drag. Then there is our desire to do what is right and to honor God. That is pulling us in the opposite direction, urging us to choose to do the right thing and to follow Jesus through our words and actions.

We are all in the battle of tug-of-war. This world doesn't want you to follow Jesus. The enemy is on an all-out assault on your soul. He wants you to give in, to just relax and let him tug you into the darkness. But God wants you to pull yourself back into the light. Do not worry. It's not a futile battle. In fact, when we invite Jesus into the fight, we will win every time. There is no strength like His. The enemy has absolutely no chance of winning when we have Jesus join us on the rope. You'll face this constant battle in your heart every day. There will be days when you give in to temptation or make a bad choice. And there is always forgiveness. But acknowledging that there *is* a battle is the first step in beating the opposing team. You're not alone in the fight. Lace up your best fighting shoes, brush off your hands, and get to work today.

Dear God, I need You in the fight against the enemy today.
There are so many opposing things pulling me
in opposite directions. Help me make the best choices
and to honor You today. Amen.

What Is Beauty?

Don't be concerned about the outward beauty of fancy hairstyles, expensive jewelry, or beautiful clothes. You should clothe yourselves instead with the beauty that comes from within, the unfading beauty of a gentle and quiet spirit, which is so precious to God.

I PETER 3:3–4 NLT

I believe that every woman is born with this innate desire to feel beautiful. That's why there is such a huge hair, makeup, and clothing industry in the United States. Women will pay hundreds and hundreds of dollars in makeup stores, in hair salons, and in brand-name clothing stores. We spend way more time in front of the mirror than boys do. We analyze our appearances, inspect our imperfections, and tweak ourselves over and over.

Beauty is an elusive creature, dear friend. You can chase it for your entire life, but you'll never feel like you've fully discovered what it is or who it looks like. Even society can't decide what beauty is. The standard of beauty changes with each edition of a magazine and each new rising star.

Beauty is a matter of opinion. Cultures around the world value different things and call them "beautiful." What's beautiful in India might not be considered beautiful here in the States. What's beautiful in your hometown or local high school may be scoffed at in another state. And the sad part is that some women spend their entire lives investing their worth in the pursuit of this elusive beauty.

In a world so focused on external appearances, it's essential to remember that God, the Creator of everything, already sees you as beautiful just the way you are, with a value that goes far beyond the surface. You are an amazing creation. Your body is a gift from God. The search for beauty could take years off your life, and it's never going to fulfill you. Love who you are, are, embrace your uniqueness, and let your beauty shine, for it reflects the incredible person God created you to be.

Dear Lord, help me turn away from the pursuit of impossible beauty. Help me to see myself as beautiful and loved. I am Your beautiful daughter. Amen.

YOUR MOVE:

Write down five beautiful things that you love about yourself.

SECTION 2

Stories from the Past

Such things were written

in the Scriptures long ago to teach us.

And the Scriptures give us hope.

ROMANS 15:4 NLT

Nowhere to Hide

The property was yours to sell or not sell, as you wished. And after selling it, the money was also yours to give away. How could you do a thing like this? You weren't lying to us but to God!

ACTS 5:4 NLT

For the next ten devotions, we'll dive into stories of people in the Bible, learning from them and applying them in our own stories. Telling lies is like being a fly caught in a spider's web. The more lies you tell, the harder you struggle, and the more trapped you become. Some of us can paint such a web of lies that we believe we have escaped the danger, but there is One who will always see right through fakes. God knows what is in your heart.

In the early days of the Christian church, two individuals named Ananias and Sapphira decided to tell a small white lie to cover up a bit of selfishness. They had sold some property, earned some money, and decided to give a partial amount of it to the local church. However, they lied to the apostles and said they had given the entire amount. When Ananias and Sapphira were caught lying to the apostle Peter, they both fell over, dead. They had lied to their friends, but more importantly, they had lied to God.

There is nowhere we can hide from Him. He knows our truest intentions.

The fate of Ananias and Sapphira was harsh, and we most likely won't get struck down dead if we lie, but the moral of the story is that God looks at lying with great displeasure. He doesn't condone telling lies, and He wants us to rise above the webs that we spin. Telling the truth is always the best way to get free of the trap we've created for ourselves. It's not always the easy path forward, but it's the path to freedom. If there is a lie that is weighing heavy on your heart, don't let it sit and fester. Don't keep lying to cover it up. You'll just end up more and more trapped. Take the path of courage and be truthful.

Dear Lord, there are always times when it seems easier to lie than to tell the truth. Help me to take the courageous path of telling the truth. Amen.

YOUR MOVE:

Spend a few minutes in prayer this morning, asking the Lord to reveal any lies that you should make right. Then take a courageous step today and tell the truth.

Consequences & Choices

So the Lord God banished them from the Garden of Eden, and He sent Adam out to cultivate the ground from which he had been made. After sending them out, the Lord God stationed mighty cherubim to the east of the Garden of Eden. And He placed a flaming sword that flashed back and forth to guard the way to the tree of life.

GENESIS 3:23–24 NLT

Adam and Eve truly did have it all. They were living in the Garden of Eden right after God created everything. They were living in the original place of perfection. They had direct access to God, and they took walks with Him. Adam and Eve experienced the close and personal relationship with God that He had created them for. That's why He made humans. These two creations were so special to God, more special than any of His other creations in the world. The man and woman had access to everything in this perfect place, except for the one tree that God asked them not to eat from.

You might know the story. The devil was disguised as a serpent, and he tempted Eve to take a bite from a fruit from the Tree of the Knowledge of Good and

Evil. Eve wanted to be like God, knowing all things as He did, so she took a bite of the fruit. She then gave it to Adam, who was standing by and watching the entire conversation without speaking up. This was the moment in history when a rip tore into God's perfect design. Sin entered the world from the choices of two people. And we are still experiencing the consequences of their choice today.

Your teenage years will show you that all of our choices have consequences, some good and some bad. You are growing into adulthood right now. It's time to start thinking about the choices that you're going to make in the next few years. Will those choices lead to good consequences? Or bad? Like Adam and Eve, could the consequences of your choices affect way more people down the road than just you? It's not easy to carry the burden of our choices. That's why we have direct access to God, who can help us make the best choices when we ask for help.

God, there are some hard decisions and choices to make right now. Help me know what choices are the best ones to take. Give me wisdom in how to move forward. Amen.

Redemption & Mercy

Rahab the prostitute is another example. She was shown to be right with God by her actions when she hid those messengers and sent them safely away by a different road.

JAMES 2:25 NLT

Rahab was a prostitute in the ancient city of Jericho. She was a Canaanite, a direct enemy of the Israelites, and living in the land that God had promised to give them. Two spies snuck into the city to do their spy things. Rahab courageously hid the spies and helped them escape when their enemies came knocking at the door. She sent the enemy soldiers on a wild goose chase, all the while aiding the Israelites in their escape. She simply asked that her family be spared from the coming takeover.

The life of a prostitute in ancient times was not a happy one. She was probably rejected by her culture. Making enough money to live was not easy for her. We don't know why she decided to help the Israelites. Maybe she saw a spark of hope in their faces that made her feel brave. Maybe she thought that the Israelites could offer her some escape. Either way, she could have been killed for protecting the spies, but she did it anyway. She was a really courageous woman.

But her story in Jericho is not the last we hear of Rahab. We later read that Rahab married an Israelite man named Salmon. They had a son together named Boaz, a name you might recognize from the book of Ruth. Boaz is the great-grandfather of King David, who led Israel to great victories. And, of course, we know that King David is the ancestor of a carpenter named Joseph, who traveled to a small town called Bethlehem with his pregnant wife, Mary, who was about to deliver the Savior of mankind.

Rahab the prostitute. A woman of disgraced character, who had lost her dignity amongst her own people, was an ancestor of Jesus Christ. She was fully redeemed by God and made into something new. Her life was forever changed because of her choice to trust the God of the Israelites. Whatever choices you've made in your life, God can redeem you. He can set you free and make you new.

Lord Jesus, what a special story Rahab's is.
You chose her to be one of Your ancestors to teach us that we can all be redeemed and made new. Thank You. Amen.

Deep Down with the Fishes

But Jonah got up and went in the opposite direction to get away from the Lord. He went down to the port of Joppa, where he found a ship leaving for Tarshish. He bought a ticket and went on board, hoping to escape from the Lord by sailing to Tarshish.

JONAH 1:3 NLT

What can we learn from dear old Jonah? You might be familiar with the story of Jonah and the whale. Jonah was a prophet of the Lord, and God told Jonah very clearly that he was to travel to the pagan city of Nineveh and tell them to turn away from their evil ways and receive mercy. But Jonah was prejudiced and cowardly. Instead of obeying God's command, Jonah hopped on a ship going in the *opposite* direction. He wanted nothing to do with the people of Nineveh. And he sure as heck wasn't going to risk his neck by going there and telling them about their impending judgment.

As we read in the book of Jonah, disobedience against God brings about consequences. A huge storm came up and threatened to overturn the ship. The sailors threw Jonah overboard in order to avoid

God's wrath. While Jonah was floating down into the sea, God sent a great fish, or a whale, to swallow him whole. Jonah survived in the fish's gut for three days (gross) until he was ready to acknowledge and express remorse for his rebellion (an action known as "repentance"), then agree to head to Nineveh.

The story doesn't end there. Unfortunately, dear old Jonah still hadn't learned his lesson. (You would think a few days marinating in stomach acid would teach a guy!) But he did obey God by preaching repentance to the people of Nineveh. We sometimes associate obeying God with obeying our parents. We probably *should* obey, but we really don't *want* to, and if it's not enforced, we probably don't *have* to. But if Jonah's story teaches us anything, it's this: God takes obedience very seriously. Don't be like Jonah. Don't wait until you've hit rock bottom before you're willing to obey. Start the walk of obedience today.

God, it's sometimes hard to obey.
You don't call us to walk the easiest path all the time.
Sometimes You call us to do something a bit scary and hard.
But You never leave us alone. Amen.

No Mistake Too Great

(For the choir director: A psalm of David,
regarding the time Nathan the prophet came to him
after David had committed adultery with Bathsheba.)
Have mercy on me, O God, because of Your unfailing love.
Because of Your great compassion, blot out the stain of my sins.

PSALM 51:1 NLT

Stop for one moment here. Take a deep breath. Hold it for four seconds. And then slowly let it out. Do that one more time.

We're going to talk about something that's hard today. And that's the reality of making mistakes.

Whatever you've done, you can receive unfailing love and forgiveness from God. The mistake may leave scars on your heart and have consequences for your future, but God is not going to abandon you or give up on you.

King David was a man who loved God with all his heart. He was the king of the Israelites. He had everything laid out before him. But he made a huge mistake. Read Second Samuel 11 for the full story. David saw a beautiful woman and decided that he wanted her as his wife, no matter the consequences and no matter the fact that she was already married. He slept with her, ruined her reputation, and then arranged for her husband to die in battle. It was probably the very lowest point in David's life. He knew he had made a huge mistake. One that would have consequences for many, many years to come.

But God has compassion even when we make huge mistakes. He never hates us. He loves us no matter what. He forgave David, and David continued to be a leader for the Israelites. He repented. His story was redeemed. And yours can be too.

Lord, it feels like my mistakes are too big to forgive. Show me how to let go of my mistakes. Forgive me for the times when I mess up. Help me learn to forgive myself. Amen.

YOUR MOVE:

Take a sheet of paper and write down that one big mistake. Then release it to God. Walk away from that mistake. Take a big permanent marker and strike through that mistake. God can erase that shame if you let Him.

The Allure of Busyness

But the Lord said to her, "My dear Martha, you are worried and upset over all these details! There is only one thing worth being concerned about. Mary has discovered it, and it will not be taken away from her."

LUKE 10:41–42 NLT

The years spent in middle school and high school can be some of the busiest times of our lives. With honors classes, sports practices, academic clubs, choir concerts, dance competitions, yearbook committee—the days can be packed. Your calendar may be filled to the brim with lessons, classes, practices, and endless homework assignments. Even weekends can be filled with football games, band competitions, and more. Many students become so immersed in their schedules and the whirlwind of activities that they rarely find time to rest. Rest? What's that?

Maybe you want to find time to spend with God, but it's so hard on top of *everything else* that is calling for your time and attention. You're probably just living each week trying to get to the weekends. But don't allow busyness to suck you into the chaos vortex that so many people are in. Busyness is a very effective tool of the devil. It keeps you from spending time with God, from praying, from attending church, and from caring for the spiritual lives of your friends.

Mary and Martha were sisters and close friends of Jesus. They hosted all of the disciples at their house, which was a huge honor in their culture. While Martha was working in the kitchen to prepare the meal, Mary was sitting at Jesus's feet, listening to His teaching. When Martha erupted in anger at Mary's "laziness," Jesus reminded Martha that so many things in life are empty and trivial, and in the grand scheme of things, it just plain doesn't matter. What *does* matter is how we live our lives and whether we live them for Jesus. Mary had it right. Instead of worrying about the to-do list and everything she *should* be doing, she took the time to sit with her Savior and learn from Him.

Dear Jesus, help me to set aside time in my calendar for You.
Help me to put aside the allure of busyness
and take hold of what really matters: You. Amen.

Obedience Like Noah's

So Noah did everything
as the Lord commanded him.
GENESIS 7:5 NLT

Noah was a typical guy living in difficult times. All over the world, people had turned away from God and had started to do really evil things. God knew that the world needed to be wiped out for a clean start. We don't know much about Noah before the flood, only that he was a righteous man and that God favored him. God had a pretty big task to ask of Noah. He told him to build a giant (and I mean *giant*) boat. God was planning on flooding the whole earth. I can just imagine being Noah. Where would I even begin? What would people think if I started spending all of my time constructing a giant boat when we lived nowhere near a lake or body of water?

The Bible doesn't specifically say what other people thought about Noah, but I think we can take a guess. They probably thought he was a lunatic. Not only did he worship a God they didn't believe in, but this God of his also told him to give up his entire livelihood to start building a massive ark to prepare for a "flood." It's so unbelievable of a tale, yet Noah obeyed. He didn't even argue. Twice the Bible says, "So Noah did everything exactly as the Lord had commanded him" (Genesis 6:22; 7:5). Noah simply obeyed. He didn't question. He didn't hesitate. He just did it.

What if we had faith and obedience like Noah's? Of course he was scared! Of course he doubted himself. Of course he wondered if he had gotten it right. People probably mocked him when year after year went by and no rains came. I wonder what Noah's family thought. Were they with him 100 percent? Did they wonder if their husband or father had gone nuts? Regardless of the crazy circumstances and command, Noah obeyed God, and he was blessed for his obedience.

Jesus gives us two commandments to live by: love God and love people. These two tasks may seem easy, but they are really hard to obey all the time. Today, think of having obedience like Noah's. How can you obey God wholeheartedly today?

Dear God, You ask us to be obedient to You and Your commandments. Help me to walk in obedience. I want to live my life for You today. Amen.

The Pain of Betrayal

At that moment the Lord turned and looked at Peter.
Suddenly, the Lord's words flashed through Peter's mind:
"Before the rooster crows tomorrow morning,
you will deny three times that you even know Me."
And Peter left the courtyard, weeping bitterly.

LUKE 22:61-62 NLT

Jesus had twelve best friends who traveled with Him during the years of His ministry. They ate together, walked together, and lived life together. Many of the teachings that Jesus offered the world came through His conversations with these twelve men. Of the twelve men, there were three who had an even closer friendship with Jesus: Peter, James, and John. They were His besties. His "ride or die" guys whom He called upon often to go above and beyond the others. Peter especially had a very strong friendship with Jesus. He was one of the first disciples Jesus called to follow Him and had been with Him from the beginning.

When Jesus was arrested and taken for trial, Peter followed along. Three times, people accused Peter of being one of the disciples, and he lied each time.

Instead of sticking up for his best friend, he betrayed Jesus to save himself. And how did Jesus respond? Well, He forgave him. And eventually, He reinstated him as a leader in the church and as His close friend.

Have you ever had a friend betray you? Maybe they leaked a secret or abandoned you? Are you still holding a grudge? Maybe it's time to to consider forgiveness. After all, Jesus walked the earth to show us how to live. He forgave Peter, and so many others. Is it your time to follow His example and choose the path of compassion?

Dear Jesus, I can't imagine the pain You felt when Peter betrayed You. But still, You forgave him. Help me learn to forgive like You do. Amen.

YOUR MOVE:

If something stirred in your heart today, take action. Apologize if you were the betrayer. Forgive if you were the betrayed. Follow in Jesus's steps today.

Hidden Secrets

"I don't have a husband," the woman replied. Jesus said, "You're right! You don't have a husband—for you have had five husbands, and you aren't even married to the man you're living with now. You certainly spoke the truth!"

JOHN 4:17-18 NLT

Women were not respected in the days when Jesus lived. Women were considered property, owned by their fathers or husbands, made for childbearing and raising kids and little else. It was a hard time to be a female. But Jesus consistently ignored the customs of His time and lifted up women from their oppression. He showed particular favor and kindness to women. He wanted everyone to know that God views women differently than how society viewed them.

Jesus ministered to one particular woman who was the lowest of the low. She was a Samaritan, and Jews and Samaritans hated each other. A Jewish man like Jesus would never have talked to a Samaritan, much less a Samaritan *woman*! But it goes a level beyond that. This woman was ostracized by her own community. She had left a trail of men behind her. The other Samaritan women would have nothing to do with someone like her. She was the lowest of the low. The dirt under the feet of a Jewish man. But Jesus saw her. He saw everything about her, including her worst secrets.

We might think we're doing a good job of hiding our issues and sins from everyone else. Maybe you have a long list of things that you've done wrong that you keep locked away. But we can't hide anything from God. Jesus looked right past her mask and saw her deepest secrets. He knew exactly what she had done in her past. And yet, He had deep compassion for her. He offered her a chance at redemption. A second chance. He lifted her up from the pit of her own making and gave her a path to a new life.

Is there something you need to confess? Do you need God to open up all your darkest secrets and lay them out? He already knows them. But right now, you can ask for forgiveness and be redeemed, just like the woman at the well.

Jesus, thank You for showing kindness to women.
Thank You for having compassion on all of us
and for seeing our darkest secrets and loving us anyway.
I ask for forgiveness from all my sins today. Amen.

Drowning in Doubt

Then He said to Thomas, "Put your finger here,
and look at My hands. Put your hand into the wound
in My side. Don't be faithless any longer. Believe!"
"My Lord and my God!" Thomas exclaimed.
Then Jesus told him, "You believe because you have seen Me.
Blessed are those who believe without seeing Me."

JOHN 20:27–29 NLT

The disciple Thomas has gotten a bad rap from Christians for centuries. In fact, he's been called "Doubting Thomas" by church leaders for generations. We have poked fun at this man for refusing to believe that Jesus had been raised from the dead. After the crucifixion, the disciples had fled and hidden for fear of their lives. They were lost and leaderless. When Jesus rose from the dead, He appeared to Mary Magdalene and to His disciples. Thomas wasn't with them when they saw Jesus for the first time, and he refused to believe. He famously said that he would not believe in a resurrected Jesus until he could feel the nail wounds in Jesus's hands and the spear wound in Jesus's side. In short, he wanted undeniable proof that Jesus was alive.

Why didn't Thomas believe his friends? He had heard from Jesus's own mouth that He would come back from the dead. They all had heard this. He had followed Jesus for years and trusted Him. His friends were probably crying and laughing with joy after seeing Jesus alive again, but still, Thomas did not want to believe. It was too difficult for him to hope and trust.

The truth is, it is easier to doubt than to trust. Doubting Thomas earned his name, but truly, he is all of us. We all have doubts about our faith. Sometimes we read something in the Bible that seems far-fetched or crazy, and that little voice inside of us whispers, "How can this be true?" We see all the horrible things happening in the world, and we ask ourselves, "How can God be real in all of this?" Every one of us should be called Doubting Thomas at some time in our lives. And you know what? It's okay to doubt! But we can still trust in the midst of our questions. God *is* real, and Jesus *did* come back from the dead. He is big enough to handle your questions.

God, I sometimes have so many questions and doubts about my faith. I'm just like Thomas. Help me to put aside my doubts and trust in You today. Amen.

SECTION 3

A Flood of Emotions

There has never been the slightest doubt in my mind that the God who started this great work in you would keep at it and bring it to a flourishing finish on the very day Christ Jesus appears.

PHILIPPIANS 1:6 THE MESSAGE

Tick, Tick, Tick

Understand this, my dear brothers and sisters:
You must all be quick to listen,
slow to speak, and slow to get angry.

JAMES 1:19 NLT

Have you seen the Disney movie *Inside Out* (the first one)? It's about a middle-school girl and the emotions that live in her head. There's Joy, Sadness, Fear, Disgust, and Anger. The emotions operate a control board in her brain and respond to various events that happen in the girl's life. One of my favorite characters is Anger. He's usually in the background, minding his own business, until he's triggered. And then, in an instant, he explodes.

What is funny in an animated movie is actually pretty accurate to what emotions are like for teenagers. Sometimes it *does* feel like there are tiny emotion characters in our heads, fighting over who gets control at that moment. Hormones make life even harder because it feels like your emotions are joining together to battle against you. How do we take control back from our own emotions?

Let's talk about that little red guy in the background. Anger. All of us have anger that sometimes spews when we least expect it. We all have a little bomb inside our minds that is slowly ticking down to our next explosion. Our anger usually erupts around those we love most: our parents, our siblings, our teammates, and our closest friends. You may often give the excuse, "I can't help it. It just comes out."

What does the Bible say about anger? First, the writer James doesn't tell us to "never, ever, *ever* have anger." He says, "You must all be quick to listen, slow to speak, and slow to get angry" (James 1:19). Do those attributes describe you? Or have you been called a "hothead"? Anger is an emotion that we all experience and have to process. It doesn't have to control you. You have the power to slow your anger. Before you let the little red guy erupt, take a few deep breaths and say a prayer. Ask the Lord to help you calm your anger. Be slow to speak. Don't spew the first words that enter your head. Those can be super-hurtful to others. Take a moment. Slow down. And restart.

Lord, I don't want to be controlled by my anger.
Please help me learn how to process my emotions
in a healthy way like James describes. Amen.

Where Is Your Focus?

Don't shuffle along, eyes to the ground,
absorbed with the things right in front of you. Look up,
and be alert to what is going on around Christ—
that's where the action is. See things from His perspective.

COLOSSIANS 3:1-2 THE MESSAGE

The average attention span for humans in the year 2000 was around 12 seconds. By the year 2015, the average attention span had reduced to 8.25 seconds. For context, the average attention span of a goldfish is around 9 seconds.[1] In short, goldfish are currently beating humans in how long they can focus on one specific task without getting distracted.

Technology has done something that very few other things have been able to do: capture our complete and total focus. Our worlds are loud. We have TVs on for background noise, phones buzzing, video games sucking us in to other realities . . . making it hard to hear ourselves think or feel anything deeply.

Today, ask yourself these questions: Where is my focus? How much time am I spending on screens? If I wanted to take a break from my devices, could I?

1 https://www.clearstepsrecovery.com/addiction-recovery-blog/average-human-attention-span-by-age

If the true answers to these questions make you a little scared, you're not alone. But you *can* take control of those controlling little screens. Try setting limits on how much time you spend on your screens each day, or make it a priority to hang out with friends in real life. Swap some of that screen time for things that lift your spirit, like reading your Bible, or just having some quiet time to connect with God. When you shift your focus to Jesus, you'll find a deeper sense of peace that is so much more fulfilling than anything a screen can offer.

Jesus, help me to choose You over all other distractions.
I need Your strength to shut out the noise.
My focus will be on You today. Amen.

YOUR MOVE:
Turn off notifications on your phone for ten minutes. Set a timer. Put your phone on the other side of the room and sit with God in prayer. You can do it!

The Battle

Don't worry about anything; instead, pray about everything.
Tell God what you need, and thank Him for all He has done.
Then you will experience God's peace,
which exceeds anything we can understand.
His peace will guard your hearts and minds
as you live in Christ Jesus.

PHILIPPIANS 4:6–7 NLT

We're going to talk about a hard topic today—mental health. Before we jump in, know this: if you struggle with your mental health, you are not alone. Mental health battles are not often talked about, but they are extremely common. One in five teen girls between the ages of thirteen and seventeen experienced major depression within the last year. One in three teens has symptoms that indicate an anxiety disorder.[1]

I started my own mental health journey while in my middle-school and high-school years. I suffered from severe insomnia, anxiety attacks, and depression. I felt hopeless and isolated, like I was standing behind a sheet of glass, watching my peers enjoy life while I floundered in my own internal pain.

However, I know something now that I didn't know

1 https://adolescentwellnessacademy.com/teen-mental-health-facts-and-statistics/

when I was your age: You don't have to stay in that pit forever. There are so many resources available to you. If you feel like you're in a battle that can't be won, start with these steps:

1. **Tell someone.** Talk to a trusted adult like your parents, a small group leader at church, or your school counselor.

2. **Keep fighting.** It may take time to see improvements, but there will be brighter days ahead.

3. **Talk to God.** God knows you inside and out. He is ready to listen to your hurts and fears and feelings. Pour them out to Him.

God, sometimes I feel like my mind is my own worst enemy.
I wonder if I'll ever feel happy again.
But You promise to give me peace when I need it.
I need Your peace and strength today. Amen.

Overcoming Fear

God is our refuge and strength,
always ready to help in times of trouble.
So we will not fear when earthquakes come
and the mountains crumble into the sea.
Let the oceans roar and foam.
Let the mountains tremble as the waters surge!

PSALM 46:1–3 NLT

Do you have any "squeal and run away" kind of fears, such as snakes, spiders, heights, or clowns? You know the ones—they can be debilitating, cold-sweat-inducing, nightmare-headlining kinds of fears. When confronted with these, it's easy to allow our fears to become all-consuming. Many of us who grapple with these fears plan ahead just in case we encounter one of these daunting situations. We take a stick with us on hiking trips for possible snakes, we make sure not to look down when finding ourselves higher up than expected, or we keep out a vacuum with a long attachment for any creepy crawlers who might show up.

And what about deep-seated fears that keep you up at night? Are you afraid of the future? Afraid of saying the wrong thing in front of your friends? Afraid of failing? Or do you have some serious fears about the state of the world around you? Just as we plan for those "squeal and run away" fears, we can plan for the big ones too. How? One way is by memorizing Scripture and actually speaking it aloud or repeating it in our minds. Speak Scripture to God in prayer. He promises to stay with us always, He promises us peace, He invites us to rest in Him, He promises to give us strength, and so much more. There is power in speaking God's Word to our fears.

Lord, help me to overcome my fear today.
I ask that You would help me find courage
to face whatever lies ahead.

YOUR MOVE:

Sometimes overcoming a fear starts with a small step. What is one step you can take today to conquer a fear that you have?

Green-Eyed Monster

A peaceful heart leads to a healthy body;
jealousy is like cancer in the bones.

PROVERBS 14:30 NLT

Have you ever heard the phrase "green-eyed monster"? For a long time, jealousy has been associated with the color green. It actually traces all the way back to Shakespeare's *Othello*. He symbolizes jealousy as a green-eyed monster, constantly feeding itself by its own "meat." The monster would keep growing and growing until it devoured its victim whole.

A little morbid, sure. But the symbolism is actually really profound.

Jealousy starts off as a simple thought. *I wish I had hair like hers.* Then, the more we think about it . . . *I can't have hair like hers. It isn't fair.* And then, it goes a little further. *No matter what I have to do, I'm going to get hair like hers.* Then we pursue that jealous thought. We become obsessed with what others have that we don't. The moment we have those shoes or dye our hair or buy that name-brand handbag, someone else walks by, and we instantly start chasing something else that we don't have. It's an endless cycle that only leaves us with a bitter heart and frustration toward the world.

Even the richest people in the world are jealous of someone. Nothing on this earth will ever cure you of jealousy. Proverbs 14:30 states, "A peaceful heart leads to a healthy body; jealousy is like cancer in the bones." How does cancer work? It starts small, but if it's not caught early, it will grow and grow, spreading to the whole body. Do you often get jealous of other people? Do you find yourself wishing you were different or had someone else's life?

Stop that weed at the root! Don't allow the green-eyed monster to start its warpath. Instead, focus your heart and mind on what you *do* have. You have so many amazing people and moments in your life. No one can be *you*. Why would you want to be anyone else? You're so incredibly loved and special. So the next time you start feeling that green-eyed monster stirring, give it a pat and remind it of all the amazing gifts God has given you.

Dear Jesus, thank You for everyone and everything You've put in my life. Help me to center my focus on gratitude and peace instead of jealousy. Amen.

Have Courage & Be Kind

Since God chose you to be the holy people He loves, you must clothe yourselves with tenderhearted mercy, kindness, humility, gentleness, and patience. Make allowance for each other's faults, and forgive anyone who offends you. Remember, the Lord forgave you, so you must forgive others.

COLOSSIANS 3:12-13 NLT

In the live-action *Cinderella* remake, there is one quote that sticks out, from Cinderella's mother. She says, "Have courage, and be kind." Just a sweet little phrase in a sweet movie. But it's actually pretty deep. In this world we live in, kindness is a lost art. People are not kind to one another. People aren't even polite these days. We are all so consumed with our own personal woes and worries that we aren't even aware of everyday people walking by us who might need an act of random kindness.

Jesus was kind to everyone. He showed attention and kindness to the people in His culture whom no one wanted to be around. He sought them out. He smiled at them. He healed them. He made them feel worthy. There are people in pain all around us. We can't solve the world's problems, but we can learn to be kind and follow in Jesus's footsteps. Today's verse teaches us a few ways to be kind. Be tenderhearted. Merciful. Forgiving. Patient. When you see another kid sitting alone at lunch, show some kindness and invite them to sit with you. When you see kids picking on someone else, have courage and stick up for them. People will be shocked by your actions, but it will show them that you are different.

Lastly, kindness to others also extends to showing kindness to yourself. If you've ever looked in the mirror and berated yourself in your mind, imagine saying those exact words to your best friend. Would you ever treat your friend the way you treat yourself? Would you tell her that she's ugly? Fat? Short? Stupid? Of course not! You'd be a terrible friend! So, why do we speak that way to ourselves?

Kindness starts with modeling how Jesus lived.

Jesus, it's not easy to be kind.
Open my eyes to different opportunities to show someone,
even a stranger, a moment of kindness. Amen.

YOUR MOVE:
Look for two opportunities to show someone kindness today.

Healing Tears

Then Jesus wept.

JOHN 11:35 NLT

The shortest verse in the Bible is John 11:35. It has three simple words, easy to pass over if you're reading too quickly. But think about that for a second. Jesus was fully God and fully human. If Jesus cried here on earth, that means the God of the universe experiences deep emotion, just like us. Jesus felt deep sadness at times during the years of His ministry. In this chapter, His close friend Lazarus had died. He had arrived too late, and they had already closed His friend's body up in a tomb. If you have read this story before, you know the ending: Jesus raises Lazarus up from the dead. He already knew what He was planning to do. There was no reason for Jesus to cry because He knew His friend would shortly return to life. But He allowed Himself to feel the grief and sadness in that moment. He modeled something to us: emotions are not our enemy.

God created tears for a reason. They serve a true purpose (other than making your eyes puffy and your nose run). When we cry emotionally, our body purges toxins out, elevating our mood and reducing stress.[1] Crying helps us relate to one another and empathize. We should never feel ashamed of our tears. Jesus was not ashamed of His. Some of us have experienced greater depths of sadness in our lives than others. But everyone will experience grief and sadness at some point. If you are in a season of sadness right now, that's perfectly okay. Cry it out. Let the tears fall. Make sure you have people surrounding you and walking with you through it. Seasons are just that—seasons. They don't last forever. God understands how you feel. He has felt it Himself and feels deep emotions just like us.

Walking through pain is sometimes the only way we can heal. You are growing stronger with every tear you shed. God is walking beside you every step of the way. He knows every tear you've cried, and He is ready with arms open, waiting for you to go to Him for comfort. Take it one step at a time.

Jesus, thank You for showing us that it's okay to cry.
My tears are a creation meant to help me.
I need You to help me get through this season of sadness
or any future sadness I encounter. Amen.

1 Therese J. Borchard, "7 Good Reasons to Cry: The Healing Property of Tears," May 29, 2011. https://psychcentral.com/blog/7-good-reasons-to-cry-the-healing-property-of-tears#4

Joy That Lasts

*I pray that God, the source of hope,
will fill you completely with joy and peace
because you trust in Him. Then you will overflow
with confident hope through the power of the Holy Spirit.*

ROMANS 15:13 NLT

There is a big difference between joy and happiness. If you walked up to any of your friends and asked them what they wanted most in life, many would say, "To be happy." The pursuit of happiness is a right listed in the Declaration of Independence. Happiness is the ultimate goal for most people in the world. So, why do so few people actually seem happy?

It's pretty simple. Happiness is fleeting. Joy is eternal. Happiness is drawn from our life circumstances. Joy is pulled from the heart of God. Happiness is dependent on things going our way. Joy is constant no matter what happens in our lives. So, how do we pursue lasting joy instead of temporary happiness?

True joy comes from resting in the knowledge of who God is and whose we are. We are God's beautiful daughters. He has a plan for each of us, and there is a purpose for us here on the earth. When we trust in God as Romans 15:13 states, we can have confidence, hope, joy, and peace. Joy relies less on what we do and more on what God has done for us. When we transfer our thoughts from, "How do I make myself happy?" to "God has given me such a beautiful life," we change our mindsets and our hearts. There will be many times in your life when hard things happen. But the beauty of following Jesus is that we can choose joy even in those hard seasons. Our circumstances might take us to the heights of mountaintops and then down into the darkest valleys, but God never changes. And because He never changes and His goodness never fades, our joy doesn't have to change either.

If you're tired of chasing that momentary instant of happiness, ask yourself this: What have you been pursuing? Have you been pursuing temporary moments? Or eternal joy through trusting God?

Jesus, I want to learn how to experience lasting joy in my life.
I put my trust in Your goodness today.
Thank You for gifting me with such a beautiful life. Amen.

The Strength to Forgive

Then Peter came to Him and asked, "Lord, how often should I forgive someone who sins against me? Seven times?" "No, not seven times," Jesus replied, "but seventy times seven!"

MATTHEW 18:21–22 NLT

Forgiveness seems like an easy thing to do until we experience a true, hurtful betrayal. When someone hurts us or mistreats us, it's human nature to want to hold a grudge or harbor hatred against them. But Jesus tells us to step away from our human nature and forgive. Forgiveness is not ignoring the betrayal or saying that it was okay. Sometimes, people do awful things to other people, and it isn't okay. But forgiveness is for *you*, not them. Forgiveness is more than just simply speaking the words, "I forgive you" when you don't mean it. It's a release from your very heart, giving up your anger and giving it to God. If there is a need for justice, God can handle that for you. There's no need for you to want revenge or payback.

Forgiving is a hard thing to do. Some people in our lives have wounded us to our very core. Some of those wounds will hurt for many years to come. Jesus tells us to forgive over and above what we might think. Sometimes we might have to forgive someone 490 times in our hearts before we really start to believe it. But forgiveness is not just an act of obedience; it's an act of healing. It's a way to turn a corner and move on from the hurt. Forgiving someone allows us to cut out that root of bitterness and release that pain to God. Sometimes broken relationships can't be mended. But other times, forgiveness is the first step toward reconciliation. Don't hold on to your bitterness. Let God step into the messy places on your behalf. The first step for you is to forgive the person and allow God to move. Jesus forgave Peter, the man who denied Him three times and abandoned Him. Whom do you need to forgive?

Jesus, help me strengthen myself to forgive.
You know each and every hurt I have on my heart.
I need Your help to be strong enough to forgive. Amen.

YOUR MOVE:
If you are having a hard time with forgiving someone, talk to a trusted mentor, a church volunteer, or a parent.

When We Feel Pain

Yet what we suffer now is nothing compared to the glory He will reveal to us later.

ROMANS 8:18 NLT

We've discussed lots of different emotions in this section. We've talked about anger and sadness, but what about when we experience pain and grief? Pain is an inevitable reality of living. The Bible is not a guidebook for a life of happiness. It doesn't promise a pleasurable, painless existence. That kind of life is a fairy tale. Instead, the Bible is full of people who experienced deep grief and heartbreaking pain. It's full of betrayal, heartache, the death of loved ones, financial ruin, martyrdom, murder, and more. The apostle Paul was beaten, whipped, shipwrecked, bitten by a snake, and thrown in prison. Ten of the eleven remaining disciples of Jesus were killed for their faith. But instead of looking at the Bible as simply depressing, we should look at it as a map for strong people who carried on through their pain.

How did the people in the Bible survive pain?

1. **They never lost hope.** Hope is an effective salve for deep pain. We have hope in a good God who never changes, no matter how hard our circumstances or how great our losses are. He's always there for you.

2. **They never gave up.** Paul writes in Romans 5:3–4 that hard times build endurance and character. Whatever pain you're experiencing now, God is going to use it to make you a stronger you. Don't give up.

3. **They didn't do it alone.** Pain is something that ties all of humanity together. The people in the Bible understood that pain and grief drew them together. If you are in a season of grief or pain, find trusted people who can help you carry the burden.

God, sometimes the pain in my life feels too heavy to bear.
But I don't have to bear it alone.
I need You to give me hope and perseverance.
Thank You. Amen.

SECTION 4

Relational Creations

Friends come and friends go,

but a true friend sticks by you like family.

PROVERBS 18:24 THE MESSAGE

Made for Relationships

Then the Lord God said, "It is not good for the man to be alone. I will make a helper who is just right for him."

GENESIS 2:18 NLT

God created a paradise in the Garden of Eden. It had everything that a person could ever dream of right there. There was no need to hunt or forage or work in a field. No hurts or pain or evil. It was absolutely perfect. But God had something extremely special in store for the last finishing touch. He made a man, Adam, and gave him dominion over all the animals in the garden. But . . . hmm . . . something still wasn't quite right. There was something missing in this perfect paradise.

Woman!

God said, "It is not good for the man to be alone" (Genesis 2:18). Can you imagine a world with no women? Part of me shudders to even think about it. It wasn't until God had created Eve that He sat back and rested after creating the entire universe. He knew that one human alone would not work. God created us to need relationships and time with others. That desire to be relational is what draws us to relationship with God.

Some of you might be strong introverts, and you might prefer time alone over large gatherings. That's just fine. But there will always be a deep need in all our hearts for community, for friendships . . . to be *known* by others. If humans weren't innately wired this way, we'd all be hermits off living in the woods. But instead, we come together for huge sporting events, school classes, and concerts. Something deep inside of us longs to be with people and to get to know them on a heart level. It's a truly wonderful gift to be human and to have the ability to care so deeply for one another. You were made to have deep relationships with other people. God put you in your family, around your friends, and in your school for a specific reason. Are you leaning into all the relationships He's put before you? Or are you keeping to yourself and not attempting to forge deeper connections? Taking an initial step to be relational requires some bravery, but the rewards of relationship are life-giving to your soul.

Dear God, show me the different people
in my life whom I can go deeper with.
Thank You for creating me to be a relational creature.
I am so glad I get to have a relationship with You. Amen.

Lonely Days

God places the lonely in families;
He sets the prisoners free and gives them joy.
But He makes the rebellious live in a sun-scorched land.

PSALM 68:6 NLT

In the last devotion, we talked about how each of us is made to have deep relationships with other people. It's in our DNA to desire connection. So, what do we do when that longing and desire is unmet? What do we do when we feel exceptionally alone in the world?

Many people go through seasons of deep loneliness during their teenage years, spending evenings and weekends alone binge-watching shows and eating cookie dough straight from the carton. It can be a challenging time, especially for those who move to an entirely new city. It may feel as though you've been dropped off on a deserted island, with no means of support. The desire for companionship is strong, but shyness can make stepping into the unknown and reaching out to others difficult. Keep in mind, though, nothing lasts forever. The lonely days will pass. Take the opportunity to pour into the relationships that you do have. Invest in your siblings. Spend quality time with your parents. Message a friend you haven't spoken to in a while and see how they are doing. Who knows?

Maybe the lonely days will prompt you to reach out to kids in your school or community with whom you would never have imagined being friends.

When you feel at your very loneliest, that's when you realize how close God actually is. The truth is: You're never alone. Even if no single human being is around you, even if you feel like nobody understands you or cares, God absolutely sees you. And He loves you more than all the people in the world combined. Sometimes the lonely days are just the catalyst for a true understanding of God's nearness.

Dear God, thank You for caring about the lonely.
Sometimes I feel like I'm all alone on a desert island.
Please bring me some true friends to encourage me. Amen.

Opposing Bullies

"The second is equally important:
'Love your neighbor as yourself.'
No other commandment is greater than these."
MARK 12:31 NLT

Some moments in your life stick to you like glue, never to be forgotten. I was thirteen, gangly and awkward, with braces and gaps in my teeth. My acne had taken over, and I had to wear my sister's old clothes to school, which were *so* out of fashion. Seventh grade was the first year that cliques formed in my junior-high school. All of the friends I had had since childhood starting caring about what others thought, gossiping and picking on others to keep the attention off of them. That desperate feeling to fit in consumed every single one of my classmates. There was one girl who went out of her way to make my life miserable. Let's call her Sue.

I walked into the lunchroom late. My friends and I always sat at one table in the cafeteria. Except this time, Sue had meticulously selected a group of people to join us at our table, filling every seat before I arrived. I walked in, holding my lunch box, and stared at the full table. No seat for me. Sue shot me a malicious grin and waved her fingers. I sat at a table in the far corner and leaned over my lunch box so none of the other kids could see my tears.

Kids can be mean. The wounds that teenagers leave on each other can last years. How do we oppose bullies? Every situation is different. If you're being bullied, go to a teacher or principal or other adult. Bullying is not okay. I prayed that God would give me the strength to be kind to Sue. I treated her with kindness all through our high-school years. But I found new friends who truly cared about me, and I left that toxic friend group behind. Jesus commanded us to love others, but we don't have to tolerate behavior that harms our well-being. It's important to surround ourselves with people who uplift and support us, while still showing compassion to those who may not treat us well. True love includes setting healthy boundaries and recognizing when it's time to move on.

Jesus, grant me the strength to love others with kindness while helping me set boundaries and seek relationships that uplift and support me. Amen.

YOUR MOVE:

Grab a journal and a pen. Make a line down the center of the page. On the left side, write attributes of bullies. On the right side, write the attributes of someone who loves her neighbor. Who would you rather be?

Little Butterflies

Flee from youthful passions, and pursue righteousness, faith, love, and peace, along with those who call on the Lord from a pure heart.

II TIMOTHY 2:22 CSB

You know that fluttery feeling you get in your stomach? The mix of excitement and nervousness that swirls around like little butterflies in your gut? It usually indicates a new crush. As teenagers, we start to notice boys in a different light. Gone are the years of boys being annoying, bouncing balls of middle-school energy. They are starting to mature (somewhat). And some of them might even be cute! Having crushes is a normal part of maturing into adulthood. Remember that God said that Adam was not meant to be alone. He needed a companion, Eve. Deep inside of us, there's that desire to be wanted and known and loved. All of those are *good* things.

So, why are the teenage years so full of heartbreaks? Hormones are a big culprit. All those chemicals in a teenager's body are careening out of control. Also, no matter how mature you might be for your years, your brain is still in the process of developing. That means that as a teenager, you *can't* make the same decisions that you might when you're a fully developed adult.

What does the Bible say about crushes and dating? Paul writes in II Timothy 2:22 to "flee from youthful passions" and to "pursue righteousness . . . along with those who call on the Lord from a pure heart." This means that while dating can be exciting, it's important to keep your focus on what truly matters—your relationship with God. Surround yourself with friends who encourage you to stay true to yourself and your beliefs. Instead of getting swept up in the drama, take the time to build healthy, respectful relationships. Remember, the right relationship will lift you up and help you grow closer to God, rather than distract your from Him.

Lord, You know my heart, and You put the desire to be loved inside of me. I want to honor You with my dating relationships and thoughts. Help me to walk in the path You want me to walk. Amen.

Deepening Friendships

Don't leave your friends or your parents' friends and run home to your family when things get rough; better a nearby friend than a distant family.

PROVERBS 27:10 THE MESSAGE

Jesus was God in a human body, walking and talking and living with other humans. Jesus performed amazing miracles, healed sick people, and even raised people from the dead. He had awesome power that can't be matched. And yet, Jesus needed friends, too. He had twelve best friends. This friend group traveled all over, lived together, and experienced life together. If Jesus, the God of the universe, needed deep friendships, we do too. So why are friendships so hard to find and hold on to?

Having deep friendships is hard work. It takes effort, vulnerability, and open communication. But the payoff is so worth it! These type of relationships foster a sense of belonging and give you opportunities for shared joy, laughter, and experiences like none other. While there's not an exact formula for how to cultivate and maintain these strong bonds, there are some steps that might help you get started:

1. **Be a friend to all.** Are you being picky and judgmental about whom you spend time with? If we limit our circle to people who act like us, look like us, or talk like us, we aren't giving God the opportunity to surprise us with friends.

2. **Sacrifice your time.** Friendships take time to build and develop. Investing in friendships requires setting aside your own selfish schedule and spending time with people.

3. **Take brave steps.** Ask someone new to grab coffee, go shopping, or simply hang out. It might be scary, but chances are, they were just waiting for someone to reach out and invite them.

Jesus, I pray that You would show me whom I can be a friend to. I really want strong friendships who will point me to You. Open my eyes to new people. Amen.

When We Get Rejected

He was despised and rejected—a man of sorrows,
acquainted with deepest grief.
We turned our backs on Him and looked the other way.
He was despised, and we did not care.

ISAIAH 53:3 NLT

In the last devotion, we talked about friendships. Having deep friendships starts with taking a brave, vulnerable step most of the time. We have to put ourselves out there to invite people in, and that often leaves us exposed to the dreaded possibility: rejection. What if they don't want to spend time with us? Or what if we get rejected by a boy we like? Sometimes intense rejection can come from a peer when we try to talk about Jesus.

Whether it's from a friend, a boyfriend, or someone else in our lives, rejection *hurts*. Many people immediately close off and withdraw after getting rejected because our innate human nature is to self-protect after a wound. We don't want to endanger ourselves by trying again. Instead, we give up and hide away, content to close off and push everyone away.

Many teenagers seek acceptance in friend groups or places where they shouldn't after getting rejected by others. *Maybe if those people don't want me, this group over here will accept me, and I can look past their bad decisions or the potential danger they bring.* "Bad" kids are rarely bad at their core. They're wounded souls who desperately sought acceptance in the wrong places, usually because they experienced the worst sort of rejection from their friends, community, or even their own family.

Rejection oftentimes leads to bitterness, then to anger, then to full-out resentment, and it can end in rebellion. Don't fall into this pattern. Instead, let's look at the life of Jesus. He never wronged anyone. He helped others. He offered a life of forgiveness and purpose. And yet, Isaiah 53:3 says, "He was despised and rejected . . . we turned our backs on Him." That sounds like the ultimate rejection. But Jesus didn't withdraw or seek out acceptance in the wrong places. Instead, He forgave. He keeps forgiving us, no matter how many times we reject Him. And the best part? He never, ever gives up.

Jesus, I'm so sorry we have rejected You over and over again.
I want to learn how to forgive those who have rejected me.
Help me to keep trying to put myself out there
in spite of those rejections. Amen.

The Purpose of Parents

Children, obey your parents because you belong to the Lord, for this is the right thing to do.

EPHESIANS 6:1 NLT

God, in His infinite knowledge, could have set up His creation any way that He wanted to. But He set up the world so that humans all have parents. It takes a man and a woman to create a new life, and they have a responsibility for the child that they bring into the world. God created the parent/child relationship as a mirror for His relationship with us, His children. When we have a great relationship with our parents, and they treat us in the way that God asks, it's a beautiful picture of the love of our heavenly Father for each individual, unique human being.

So, why are parents so *hard?* The simplest answer is this: Parents aren't perfect. Our relationships with our parents will never be the perfect relationship that God intended because our parents are sinful and so are we. Our parents will make mistakes. We'll make mistakes. The closest relationships in our lives have the greatest potential to deeply wound us. If your parents have wounded you, I am so sorry. It's crucial to reach out to a school counselor or trusted adult for support, as they can provide guidance and help navigate these difficult feelings.

Your parents could be separated by divorce. Maybe you're adopted and are navigating that reality. Maybe you are living in a foster care environment. Or maybe you have both your mom and dad at home with you, but there is constant fighting and tension.

In most cases, parents are our shepherds from the moment we are born to the moment we leave their home and enter the world on our own. Most parents are simply doing their best, but sometimes they make mistakes. God put you in your family for a reason. Instead of thinking of all the ways your parents are making your life *difficult*, consider this: How are you helping them in their role as parents? Do you listen to them? Obey them? Or do you battle against them every step of the way?

God, show me how to respect and honor my parents,
even when I am frustrated with them.
Thank You for giving me my parents and my family. Amen.

YOUR MOVE:

Tell your parents that you're grateful for them.

Paul & Timothy

That's why I have sent Timothy,
my beloved and faithful child
in the Lord. He will remind you
of how I follow Christ Jesus, just as
I teach in all the churches wherever I go.

1 CORINTHIANS 4:17 NLT

The apostle Paul was one of the greatest evangelists in all of history. Jesus transformed his life, and he devoted the rest of his years to telling everyone he could about Jesus and the hope that He provides. Paul was a busy guy. He constantly traveled from one place to another, sharing his beliefs and working with local churches wherever he went. The man didn't have a lot of free time. And yet, Paul still found the time to mentor a young man named Timothy.

Remember: We are created to be relational beings. Many times, God brings people into our lives to help lead us in the right direction. Mentorship is a beautiful thing, and it can bring about major life changes. Timothy was probably in his late teens when Paul met him in Lystra. Paul was amazed by the boy's immense faith and passion for Jesus, and he asked Timothy to join him on his journeys. For many years after that, Paul mentored Timothy and taught him how to be a man, empowering him to be all that he could be. Timothy went on to become a pastor of the church in Ephesus because Paul had so much trust in his leadership.

Do you have a mentor in your life? Are you actively looking for adults you want to model? If there is a woman in your church or community whom you admire, ask her to mentor you. It is such a gift to have someone older give you insights and wisdom as you grow up and make big decisions. Learning from those who have gone before you shows great maturity and initiative. Who knows? You could make a lifelong friend.

What about you? Do you hang out with girls much younger than you? Do you try to lead others and empower them in your faith? You can be a mentor-like figure in the life of a young girl. God used a young teenage man named Timothy to do amazing things. He wants to use you too.

Jesus, show me who can be a Paul-like mentor to me. Help me find a woman who can encourage and empower me in my faith. Then, show me how I can be an encouragement to someone younger than me. Amen.

Last Nerve

How wonderful and pleasant
it is when brothers live together in harmony!

PSALM 133:1 NLT

Here's the thing. Brothers and sisters should be the most amazing built-in best friends ever. You're born into the same family. You have the same upbringing. You're together all the time, and you get to make lifelong memories together. So, why, why, why are siblings so annoying?

The answer is . . . everything I just said. Siblings are with you all the time. You can't escape them until you move out of the house. Most likely, your brothers and sisters and you are all completely different people. You might not enjoy doing the same things, eating the same foods, hanging out with the same people . . . the list goes on. But, strangely enough, you would do about anything for your siblings if something bad happened or if someone was bullying them.

What should we do when our siblings get on our last nerve? Psalm 133:1 says, "How wonderful and pleasant it is when brothers live together in harmony!" Have you made an effort to live in harmony with your siblings? Do you practice patience when they don't stop talking? Do you practice selflessness when they refuse to go to the restaurant you enjoy? Do you work on forgiveness when they say something that hurts you?

Having siblings gives us great insight into how to love people unconditionally. Our families get our worst moments and our best moments. You have a front-row seat to your siblings growing and developing in their own faith journeys. And sometimes, it's not a fun process to be a part of. But they are doing the same for you. Siblings are a wonderful gift from the Lord, and we can be grateful for every moment we get to spend with them, even when we wish we could have a break from them for a bit.

No family is perfect. Siblings will test you, but they will also always be there for you through thick and thin. They're your teammates for life.

Jesus, thank You for giving me my siblings.
Help me to learn how to love them unconditionally like You do.
Show me what a gift they are. Amen.

YOUR MOVE:
Practice saying three kind things to each of your siblings today. It might shock them!

Called to Community

Let us think of ways to motivate one another to acts of love and good works. And let us not neglect our meeting together, as some people do, but encourage one another, especially now that the day of His return is drawing near.

HEBREWS 10:24-25 NLT

Whom do you spend your time with? What are your friends like? Are your friends pointing you to Jesus? Or are they dragging you away from your faith?

The people we spend our time with influence us. If you surround yourself with friends who are making bad decisions, rebelling, or not following Jesus, it's hard to keep from joining them. God made us as relational creatures, but we get to choose the people we hang out with. And the friends you have during your teenage years have the power to define you for the rest of your life. Community is important.

A lot of people try to run with the "popular" crowd during their junior-high years, and a lot of times, being a part of that crowd means openly bullying others to deflect attention away from themselves. It's true, friends often cause wounds and betrayal. But you have a choice—continue following friends who are unkind or break away and seek new friendships.

Remember, it's not about fitting in; it's about finding your place among those who celebrate who you are. Embrace the courage to break free from negativity and discover friendships that truly reflect love and support. Your worth is not determined by popularity but by the kindness you extend to yourself and others.

Look for a church community to invest in. Youth groups are wonderful places to find friends who will encourage you in your faith. Find other students who will walk alongside you as you follow Jesus. You don't have to do this alone.

God, please show me how to find
a strong community who will build me up
and encourage me to follow You.
I want to find some strong friends
who will be there for me. Amen.

From Sprout to Seedling

Grow in grace and understanding of our Master and Savior, Jesus Christ. Glory to the Master, now and forever! Yes!

II PETER 3:18 THE MESSAGE

Childhood Hurts

The Lord is close to the brokenhearted;
He rescues those whose spirits are crushed.

PSALM 34:18 NLT

We're in the section of the devotional called "From Sprout to Seedling." That is what the teenage years are. You have matured past childhood and those carefree years of being a kid, and you're emerging into the "in between" stage of life. You're not an adult yet, but you're not a kid anymore. You don't want to be considered a kid, but you're not quite developed to think entirely like an adult either. Welcome to the joys of teenage life.

It's easy to want to jump ahead and into adulthood. You may want to put your childhood behind you forever and move on, or you may want to grow up because there were some big hurts in your childhood that you believe will fade as you become an adult. Unfortunately, that's not how life works. We can't leave behind our past. There might be some tough memories that you don't want to deal with. Maybe you're afraid those memories will cause you to ask hard questions about God.

But you can start to work through your childhood hurts right now in these "in between" years. Start the journey of forgiveness and healing from those past wounds. Take the step of courage and pray about how God wants you to grow. Listen, God knows your pain and your struggles. Psalm 34:18 says, "The LORD is close to the brokenhearted; He rescues those whose spirits are crushed." God cares. He is ready to help you heal and move confidently forward in your life. Is there someone you need to forgive? Is there a friend to whom you need to go back to and apologize? Are there hard moments that scared you as a child that you want to talk with someone about? Take those courageous steps today and begin your healing journey. You'll find that the healing journey is a lifelong process with the Lord. It might be time for you to start.

God, I don't like thinking about those childhood hurts.
But I want to heal and move on.
Help me to find the right path of healing. Amen.

YOUR MOVE:

If something popped into your mind while reading this, take action. Talk to a parent, trusted leader, pastor, or counselor and take a big, brave step.

Growing Pains

When I was a child, I spoke and thought
and reasoned as a child. But when I grew up,
I put away childish things.

I CORINTHIANS 13:11 NLT

Growing up is hard, and being a teenager is no joke. Your body is constantly changing and developing. Your internal chemical makeup is morphing each day, taking you on a roller-coaster ride of emotions. Temptations are becoming harder and harder to ignore. You want to do the right thing, but why is it always so hard?

Be kind to yourself. This is a difficult season for most people your age. Your story and your experiences are unique to you. No one else can truly understand what you're going through because they aren't you! But God knows. As you continue to grow and change, use this time in your life to develop a close relationship with Him. Develop habits and a routine of spending time with God each day. Make an effort to pull your Bible out to read His Word and listen to what God has to say to you.

No one expects you to be perfect in this life. It's not possible. As you grow and change, embrace who God made you to be. Don't chase after perfection.

Don't chase after temporary things like fashion trends, beauty tutorials, and popularity. Those things are fickle friends, and they won't stick once you grow out of high school.

Who do you want to become in your life? These are vital years. Who you become right now will shape who you will be for the rest of your life. Not to mention, teenagers are important to this world and society today. Your generation shows a lot of passion for things that matter to them. You like to stay connected to the world and to each other. You love to laugh and enjoy each moment.

It can be so easy to want to skip this season of life and just get to the adult years. But this is a special time for you. God is doing a work right *now*, even when those growing pains are uncomfortable.

Jesus, thank You for these special teenage years. You are doing something really important in my life right now. Show me the ways that I can prepare myself for the future You have for me. Amen.

Don't Struggle in Silence

Share each other's burdens,
and in this way obey the law of Christ.

GALATIANS 6:2 NLT

Take another moment and reread today's verse. "Share each other's burdens." We were all taught as children that we need to share, but who would ever want to share someone else's burdens? And yet, God wants us to carry the loads of others. That means there are people in your life who can help you carry your own burdens too. No one can ever fully understand your personal experience. They aren't you. But they can listen, encourage, and help you.

If you are in a season of struggling, whom have you told? Are you battling your struggles all by yourself? If you don't invite others into your difficulties, then you're actually preventing them from doing what God has asked all of us to do: share the load. If you don't have any trusted adults in your life, find a local church and speak to a pastor or minister. Find a qualified counselor who will listen to you. Don't be afraid to share what's really going on in your life and in your heart.

Imagine a football game. Would the game last very long if only one player from the home team showed up to the game? No, of course not. That poor guy wouldn't last two downs. It takes a team to win a football game, and it takes a team to carry each other's hard times. Our faith is not meant to be lived out in isolation. We are supposed to help each other, just like Jesus helped so many people and cared about His friends.

Sometimes the easy road is to struggle in silence rather than open up about your pain. But take the brave path and invite trusted adults and other people into the situation. It might help you get the win that you need.

Jesus, help me to trust other people to share my burdens. Show me how to be a friend who also helps other people in their struggles. Amen.

YOUR MOVE:

Stretch out of your comfort zone and talk to someone this week. Reach out to a friend who is struggling and offer to listen and to help.

Magic Mirror, on the Wall

This is God's Word on the subject: "'As soon as Babylon's seventy years are up and not a day before, I'll show up and take care of you as I promised and bring you back home. I know what I'm doing. I have it all planned out—plans to take care of you, not abandon you, plans to give you the future you hope for."

JEREMIAH 29:10-11 THE MESSAGE

Do you remember the original Disney animated movie *Snow White and the Seven Dwarfs*? At one point the evil queen steps up to her mirror and quotes, "Mirror, mirror, on the wall, who is the fairest of them all?" Wouldn't it be nice (though slightly creepy) if we all had a mirror there to answer whatever question we have about the future? What if we could ask, with certainty, "What am I going to do after I graduate?" "Will I have a good job that I love?" "Will I have a family someday?" And then *viola!* Immediate answers! No more worried conversations with parents or stress over grades or applications to multiple colleges. You will simply know what you need to do and how to get there. Wouldn't that be amazing?

The Israelites wanted answers too. Babylon

had enslaved the Israelites, and they had been in captivity for seventy years. Their beloved Jerusalem had been sacked, and their beautiful temple had been demolished. They were a broken and wounded people because of their own sin against God. God allowed their captivity in Babylon to teach them about sin and consequences. Jeremiah wrote a letter to these captive people, informing them about God's justice and punishment, but also providing a sliver of hope for their future. Through Jeremiah, God told His people, "I'll show up and take care of you" and "I have it all planned out."

God has your future planned, and it's been written . . . since forever. Nothing you will ever do will surprise God. It's okay to feel nervous and uncertain about the future and what decisions to make. None of us has a magic mirror that tells us what to do. But we can pray and ask God to give us wisdom. We can make choices knowing that God is going to be right there with us and He already knows what we will decide. We can trust God to show us the right paths to take.

Dear God, I feel so overwhelmed with worry about the future. I don't know what is going to happen or what decisions to make. Help me find the right path to take. Amen.

Good Out of the Bad

*And we know that God causes everything
to work together for the good of those who love God
and are called according to His purpose for them.*

ROMANS 8:28 NLT

Growing up gives us the gift of looking back on our past. Once we have some years under our belts, we can start to see the pattern of God's hand working throughout our lives. Now, that doesn't mean that we should downplay the hardship and difficulties we face. You might be in a rocky season right now or maybe you've had one recently. It's never fun to go through the bad times. But after some time has passed, we're able to look back and see how God brought good out of that pain.

My aunt died in a car accident when I was eleven years old. That moment in time changed my entire life experience. My childhood ended with one phone call, and I fell into the sticky middle of still having childish emotions while experiencing grown-up suffering. For years, my family suffered from the massive loss. My aunt was a vibrant, beautiful, joyful woman whom we all adored. She had made a true mark on the world.

Now, even twenty years later, it's hard to look back and see "good" in all of that pain. Paul doesn't write in Romans 8:28 that all the bad in the world is made "good" by God. He is talking about our spiritual good, our spiritual growth, and our faith journey with God.

Now, let's think about my aunt's death through that viewpoint. My aunt's death was a tragic moment in my life. It shattered my heart to pieces, and I still feel the pain of it to this day. But God used that moment in my life and helped me spiritually grow through it. My faith matured in that season. I turned to God for help, and He answered me. He used that horrible time in my life to show me that He is always there. I don't know why my aunt died that day, but I do know that God was with me through it all. I am the woman I am today because God used my pain to help me spiritually grow from it. Where do you need to see the good in your life right now?

Jesus, I can't understand why things happen in the world or why there are bad times. But I am so thankful that You have a plan and You will help me to grow spiritually through the pain for my ultimate good. Amen.

Yearning for Respect

Dear brothers and sisters,
honor those who are your leaders in the Lord's work.
They work hard among you and give you spiritual guidance.
Show them great respect and wholehearted love because
of their work. And live peacefully with each other.

I THESSALONIANS 5:12-13 NLT

Here's the rub of the teenage years. You're nearing adulthood, and you're starting to make some big decisions in life. You're feeling more like an adult and less like a kid. Instead of hanging out at the little kid table at the family Thanksgiving dinner, you sit with the adults and laugh at all the comments they make about politics and gas prices. But . . . you're not an adult yet. You're still living with your parents and siblings. Your parents have the final word on a lot of your choices. You want to be treated like an adult, but when they disagree and push back, it can be so *frustrating.*

Have you ever wondered why it's so frustrating? Could it be that the main issue at hand is that you yearn for respect? Give your parents a little break. They birthed you. Changed your diapers. Spoon-fed you. Cleaned your cuts and scrapes. It is never easy for a parent to look at their child and realize they are about to be all grown-up. It's not easy for them to transition from being your ultimate authority to respecting your adult decisions.

So, next time your parents say "no" to your hanging out with friends late at night or ask you to babysit your younger siblings *again*, think about this: What will *earn* their respect? If it's respect and the ability to make your own adult decisions that you're looking for, that doesn't come overnight. Parents are people too. They need to see that they can trust and respect your decisions. So, don't get mad at them when they say "no." Don't go to your room and shut them out. Try this:

"Mom, Dad, I'll respect your decision on this, and I'll do what you say. Next time, can we talk about what I can do to earn your trust and respect and make this decision on my own?"

Once they pick their jaws up from the floor, you might find that they listen to you and do what you ask. Respect is a give-and-take, and it's earned.

God, I really want to be respected and trusted to make my own decisions. Help me to be patient and obey my parents in the meantime. Amen.

Such a Time As This

If you keep quiet at a time like this, deliverance and relief for the Jews will arise from some other place, but you and your relatives will die. Who knows if perhaps you were made queen for just such a time as this?

ESTHER 4:14 NLT

If you're a big fan of stories with a lot of drama, you should read the book of Esther in the Bible. It reads like a fairy tale. A handsome king is searching for a queen. A poor young woman is chosen to become queen. She goes from rags to riches, marries Prince Charming, and gets to live a dream life.

Of course, in every good story, there's a bad guy. And in this story, it's Haman. Haman was the king's right-hand man, and he hated the Jewish people. Esther was Jewish, and her relative, Mordecai, was a scribe for the king. Haman had a pretty evil idea: trick the king into ordering the execution of all the Jewish people in the land. Once the king had made an order, it was carried out. That meant that all of Esther's friends and family would be killed—including her, if the king ever found out she was Jewish.

Mordecai came to beg Esther for help. He asked her to go to the king and plead for mercy for the Jewish people. But if Esther were to approach the king uninvited, she would be killed immediately, no questions asked. Esther had to make a hard choice. Was she willing to die for her people? Mordecai asked her, "Who knows if perhaps you were made queen for just such a time as this?" (Esther 4:14).

All it takes is scrolling through a newsfeed to realize that our world is filled with challenges, conflicts, and uncertainty. But what if God placed you right where you are, right when you are, for such a time as this? He had a plan for Queen Esther, and He has a plan for you. He placed you in your town, in your family, in your school, for a reason. Perhaps the decisions you make won't affect an entire nation like Esther's, but you are uniquely placed to be an influence on your friends and family. There's a reason you're here on earth right now. What choices will you make?

God, help me to have the courage of Queen Esther. You put me here for a reason. Show me how I can use my influence to point others to You. Amen.

No Limits

Don't let anyone think less of you because you are young.
Be an example to all believers in what you say,
in the way you live, in your love, your faith, and your purity.

I TIMOTHY 4:12 NLT

Teenagers have done some amazing things in history. Louis Braille was fifteen years old when he invented the Braille reading system for the blind. Malala Yousafzai, a Pakistani female education activist, won the Nobel Peace Prize at the age of seventeen. Teenagers can change the world, and no one should underestimate what you can do.

Paul had similar thoughts. In I Timothy 4:12, he is writing a letter to his mentee, Timothy, and he says, "Don't let anyone think less of you because you are young." Timothy was a teenager when Paul took him on his first missionary journey, and he became a church leader and pastor at a very young age. Can you imagine if your pastor at your church stepped down and an eighteen- or nineteen-year-old stepped up to lead? What do you think the older people in the church would think?

But that's exactly what happened with Timothy. Paul believed in him and what he could do. His age didn't matter. What did matter was what God had done in Timothy's heart. *You* can change the world. Truly. Decisions that you make right now can affect your future and countless others' futures. If you dedicate your life to Jesus at this young age, there are no limits to what you can do for Him in your life. You don't need to have a doctorate in theology to love Jesus and want others to know Him. You have a strong, yet simple faith, and you're truly unstoppable when you get motivated for the Lord. So don't allow the evil one to lie to you about what you can accomplish. This is the beginning of a lifelong journey of endurance and obedience to God. And you can start doing some big things right now.

God, show me what You want me to do right now for You.
I am not bound by the limits of my age,
and You have a plan for me in this season. Amen.

YOUR MOVE:
Start dreaming about what you can do for Jesus right now and in the future. What are some big dreams that God has put on your heart? Write them down and date them.

A Letter to My Past Self

Get all the advice and instruction you can,
so you will be wise the rest of your life.

PROVERBS 19:20 NLT

Dear teenage me,

Everyone is awkward as a teenager. It's not just you. Those braces? They'll come off, and then you'll love your smile. Those boys? Won't be so cute in ten years. Those girls bullying you? You'll come to find out they were struggling too. That one godly friend who is sticking by you through it all? She'll be your best friend for years to come. Chances are someday you'll both have husbands and kids and laugh about all the crazy things you did as teenagers.

Love yourself. You might have acne. You might have weird teeth and braces. Your hair might be straight and greasy no matter how many times you wash it. But this won't last forever. You are beautiful just as you are, including the minor features you consider flaws. When you look in the mirror, focus on the strength in your eyes, the smile that lights up your face, and the uniqueness that makes you, you. Tell yourself positive things about your body. You are an incredible creation!

Your innocent faith is a precious thing. You don't have to try so hard to meet His expectations. God is already pleased with you and proud of you, no matter what you do now or in the future. You can just rest and be His daughter.

These teenage years may seem endless now, but they actually fly by. You are so special. You're loved more than you know. You have so many beautiful things ahead of you.

Love,
Your future adult self

God, help me to keep everything in perspective.
I have an entire life ahead of me.
This is only a season. Amen.

Wide Open

So we're not giving up. How could we! Even though on the outside it often looks like things are falling apart on us, on the inside, where God is making new life, not a day goes by without His unfolding grace. These hard times are small potatoes compared to the coming good times, the lavish celebration prepared for us. There's far more here than meets the eye. The things we see now are here today, gone tomorrow. But the things we can't see now will last forever.

II CORINTHIANS 4:16–18 THE MESSAGE

This season in your life is just that: a season. And it will pass. Before you know it, you'll be a legal adult making your own life decisions. You'll work or go to college or travel the world. Maybe you'll get married. Maybe you won't. But the future is wide open for you. Whatever your childhood or teenage years have brought, there is so much hope for the years ahead.

God is in the business of making things new. One of my favorite Bible verses is Lamentations 3:22–23 (CSB): "Because of the LORD's faithful love we do not perish, for His mercies never end. They are new every morning; great is Your faithfulness!" His mercies are new every morning. That means that whatever wrongs you did yesterday . . . whatever bad decision you made . . . or whatever pain you've experienced in your past

. . . God's mercy is like hitting a "reset" button every morning. You can start fresh. God will be faithful to walk with you as you grow from child to adult, from the small sprout you were as a child to the seedling you are now as a teenager and then finally to the beautiful full-grown tree you'll be as an adult. He is there to refresh you and help you start over each day so you can walk forward into the future with hope. Growing up is scary, but you don't have to navigate it alone.

Dear God, thank You for refreshing me each and every day.
Thank You for Your great faithfulness and promise
to be there for me always. Because of You,
I have a deep hope for the future. Amen.

YOUR MOVE:

Spend some time today dreaming about your future. What are some plans and goals you feel like God has put on your heart? How do they make you feel?

SECTION 6

Becoming Like Jesus

You can never learn that Christ is all you need, until Christ is all you have.

CORRIE TEN BOOM

In Lockstep with Jesus

Jesus spoke to the people once more and said,
"I am the light of the world. If you follow Me,
you won't have to walk in darkness,
because you will have the light that leads to life."

JOHN 8:12 NLT

If you're a member of the marching band at your school, you'll love this. I was in marching band in high school. I played French horn, twirled as a majorette, and served as drum major of the band my senior year. Band was a big part of my high-school identity. I made good friends in band, and we made many memories. Most sports athletes don't quite understand that band members give plenty of sweat and tears as well. We would practice our marching band set for hours during the heat of the summer, listening to our band director shout through a megaphone when we stepped out of line. My high school had a military marching band style, meaning that we all marched in perfect synchrony and in perfect step together. If even just one person was a tad behind, you could see that person breaking formation from the stands. We all had to march in complete lockstep for the routine to work and for the formations to wow the audience. And due to the angry band director standing on a platform above us, none of us wanted to be the one out of line.

In much the same way, we need to walk in lockstep with Jesus, right in synchrony, in tune, and on the right beat. It's so easy to get out of step when we're following Jesus. All of us will miss a beat, fall behind, or make a big mistake. But unlike my high-school self cringing when I heard my name screeched across the football field, Jesus isn't waiting to call you out for a mistake. He is walking right alongside you, patiently waiting for you to find your footing and rejoin Him in this march of life. As we become more and more like Jesus, it will be easier and easier to keep pace with Him. Then you'll be able to instruct others in how to join you.

Jesus, thank You for leading me forward into light instead of darkness. Help me to learn how to walk with You in lockstep without falling behind or stumbling. I need Your help to do it. Amen.

The Light of the Holy Spirit

"You are the light of the world—like a city on a hilltop that cannot be hidden. No one lights a lamp and then puts it under a basket. Instead, a lamp is placed on a stand, where it gives light to everyone in the house."

MATTHEW 5:14-15 NLT

When we decide to follow Jesus with our lives, He sends His Holy Spirit to live in our hearts for the rest of our lives. The Holy Spirit is that little voice in our minds that interrupts a bad thought or whispers a warning when we walk down the wrong path. The Holy Spirit is our Guide for the rest of our days. We are marked by the Holy Spirit when we decide to become Christians. And when we are pursuing a life of following Jesus, the Holy Spirit can't help but shine out of us. You'll be different from everyone else who doesn't believe in Jesus, and that's okay. Other people *should* notice that something is different about you. We are called to let the light of the Holy Spirit shine out of our hearts and radiate to all the people around us.

Jesus preached that "you are the light of the world" (Matthew 5:14 NLT). We are called to something much bigger than ourselves. If we want to become like Jesus, we need to see the world through His eyes. He loves each and every person we interact with. And He needs us to show them this love. God has tasked us with shining His light to others so they can experience this freedom for themselves.

Jesus also said that "no one lights a lamp and then puts it under a basket. Instead, a lamp is placed on a stand, where it gives light to everyone in the house" (v. 15). The light of the Holy Spirit is meant to be shared with others. Don't hide what you believe. Tell others about what Jesus has done in your life. Be kind to the people who are hard to be kind to. Be generous. Keep that lamp uncovered so the world can know the Jesus whom you know.

Jesus, thank You for giving me the light of the Holy Spirit, who walks with me and shows me the right paths to take. I want to shine my light out for the world to see. Help me do this as I go about my day. Amen.

The Unlovable

Dear friends, let us continue to love one another, for love comes from God. Anyone who loves is a child of God and knows God.

I JOHN 4:7 NLT

Think about the most evil places on earth. Maybe you're thinking about the hideout of a terrorist group. Or maybe you're imagining a war zone. Perhaps you thought about the halls of a prison where murderers await their fates. Humans are capable of so much evil. It's truly astonishing. But we are also capable of incredible love.

All of those evil places in the world are filled with people we would easily call "unlovable." They are the worst of humanity. Who would love them?

Or maybe, on a less serious note, the main bully in your school . . . pretty unlovable, right?

But God loves them. If they were the only ones left on the planet, Jesus would have died for them still, because He wants the total redemption of humanity, even those who are the most unlovable. There are many, many stories of death-row inmates coming to know Jesus. I have personally heard a story of a terrorist who saw a vision of Jesus, and he abandoned his evil mission and began to tell other terrorists about

Jesus. Even the most evil people can be redeemed.

Think about the most "unlovable" person in your life or in the community. Why is it so hard to love them? The apostle John writes in I John 4:7, "Let us continue to love one another, for love comes from God." That means when we are followers of Jesus, we do what He did—love people. Even the hardest people to love deserve to know that they can be loved no matter what. Everyone in this world is pursuing the desire to be known and loved. It's a gaping hole in all of our hearts. You have the ability to show those people that they can find that love through Jesus and heal that gaping hole. And loving the unlovable is the best way to show them that there is hope and redemption available to them, no matter what.

Jesus, I need Your help to love the unloveable. Show me what loving them looks like and give me the strength to love them, no matter what. Amen.

Note: If you are experiencing an abusive, unhealthy relationship in your life, loving someone might mean loving from a distance or loving them by setting healthy boundaries. Loving someone does not mean that we place ourselves in hurtful situations. Talk to a trusted counselor or adult in your life if this is you.

Dangerous Words

"Words are powerful; take them seriously.
Words can be your salvation.
Words can also be your damnation."

MATTHEW 12:37 THE MESSAGE

Take another moment and reread today's Scripture. This is Jesus speaking, and it might seem a bit harsh. But if you read the entire chapter of Matthew 12, it will make more sense. The Pharisees were constantly nitpicking everything Jesus said and did. They accused Him of heresy and witchcraft, and then they turned around and demanded a sign or miracle to prove that He really was the Messiah. They taught the people to follow the Law of God, but then they went and broke the laws themselves. Jesus needed to get their attention, and He did so in this passage of Scripture.

There is something that we can learn from the Pharisees. Words matter. Jesus is saying that God will judge each of us on the Day of Judgment for the words that we said in our lives. That means that every time you shout at your siblings or respond in anger to your parents, those words aren't disappearing. God hears them and remembers them. Words are really harsh weapons, and they wound deeply. So, when you're angry at your parents and speak really mean things to them without thinking, that's really hurtful to them. And, in turn, that hurts God.

It takes training to "tame the tongue." But you can start today. When you're tempted to say something you know you might regret, stop, take a deep breath, and think. Do you really mean what you're about to say? Is the purpose of those words to wound? Will you regret them later once you calm down? If the answer to any of these questions is "yes," take yourself out of the situation until you can think clearly. You could save a lot of pain if you learn now that words are dangerous when we allow them to flow without thought.

Dear God, I'm so sorry for the words that I've spoken in the past. Forgive me for those hurtful words and help me to learn how to stop and think before I speak. Amen.

YOUR MOVE:

Is there someone in your life you've hurt with your words? Do the right thing today and go apologize. No one is perfect. We'll all mess up. But we can do our best to make it right.

I'll Save You a Seat

Later, Matthew invited Jesus and His disciples to his home as dinner guests, along with many tax collectors and other disreputable sinners. But when the Pharisees saw this, they asked His disciples, "Why does your teacher eat with such scum?" When Jesus heard this, He said, "Healthy people don't need a doctor—sick people do." Then He added, "Now go and learn the meaning of this Scripture: 'I want you to show mercy, not offer sacrifices.' For I have come to call not those who think they are righteous, but those who know they are sinners."

MATTHEW 9:10–13 NLT

There is something universal about the fear of walking into a crowded cafeteria and not knowing where to sit. Let's face it, sitting alone in a lunchroom is a teenager's worst nightmare. In fact, at the beginning of the school year, you probably start comparing your class schedules with your friends to see if your lunch times line up. Then you start planning with those who have the same lunches to make sure you have a seat at the table. Am I right? And it's even scarier when you move to a new town or school—it's terrifying to walk into a cafeteria when you don't know *anyone* at that school.

Jesus always invited people to sit at His table, and He was never picky about who those people were.

In His day and age, tax collectors were the worst of the worst. And Jesus befriended a tax collector named Matthew. The Pharisees were absolutely mortified that a respected teacher like Jesus was hanging out with the scum of their society. But Jesus kindly reminded them, "Healthy people don't need a doctor—sick people do" (Matthew 9:12). Jesus wanted those Pharisees to know that the people He really needed to spend time with were the ones who were outcasts in society.

Who at your school, church, or community needs people to hang out with? Are you someone who invites everyone to sit at your lunch table? Are you willing to make new friends when you are comfortable with the friends that you have? Do you look for people on the outskirts who could be in need of a friend? Be the person who always says, "I'll save you a seat."

Jesus, thank You for teaching us about inviting everyone into our lives, no matter where they stand in social circles. Show me people who I can reach out to today. Amen.

YOUR MOVE:

Keep your eyes open for people in your school today who are sitting alone or look like they could use a friend.

The Ultimate Servant

*"And since I, your Lord and Teacher,
have washed your feet,
you ought to wash each other's feet."*

JOHN 13:14 NLT

The night before Jesus was betrayed by one of His closest friends, He had one last dinner with His twelve followers. Jesus knew what was coming for Him, and He had a few last important things to say to them before His death.

During the years that Jesus lived, they had a few customs. First, when you entered a home, the servant of the home would help you remove your sandals and then wash the dirt and grime from your feet. In this time, everyone walked everywhere, and they primarily wore sandals on their feet. So you can imagine the dirt, mud, manure, and who knows what else could be covering their shoes and feet. The lowliest of the servants had to stoop for this (pretty gross) task when guests arrived.

But Jesus grabbed a towel and a large bowl and knelt before each and every friend at the table to wash their dirty feet. One of the men, Peter, was horrified at the thought of his Lord stooping to such a lowly state to wash his disgusting feet, but Jesus scolded him for his pride. Jesus was sending a message to them. He was the Messiah of the world, God in human flesh, but He humbled Himself to the lowliest of servant positions to show His friends that He came to serve others, not Himself. After He was done with the task, He said, "Since I . . . have washed your feet, you ought to wash each other's feet" (John 13:14). Obviously, Jesus didn't mean that in literal terms. He was showing them that we are called to serve each other, even if it feels hard or humiliating in the moment. We are to follow Christ's example of how He treated His friends.

Do you often jump up to serve your parents without asking? When was the last time you cleaned your room or washed the dishes just to be a help? Take a challenge for yourself today. Model what Jesus did for His friends. He didn't do it for attention. He did it to show them how much He loved them. How can you love by serving someone today?

Jesus, You became the ultimate Servant to show us that we should serve each other. Show me how to put other people before myself, even when it's hard. Amen.

Like a Mustard Seed

"You don't have enough faith," Jesus told them. "I tell you the truth, if you had faith even as small as a mustard seed, you could say to this mountain, 'Move from here to there,' and it would move. Nothing would be impossible."

MATTHEW 17:20 NLT

Jesus was traveling through Galilee, teaching crowds of people about God and how to follow Him. A man came up to Him and asked Jesus to help his son, who was demon-possessed and often hurt himself and others. The man was desperate for a solution to an impossible situation. Some of Jesus' disciples had already tried to free the boy of the demon, but it hadn't worked. Jesus got frustrated with the disciples and the crowd around Him. He had taught them so much already, but they didn't seem to get it. He said, "You don't have enough faith . . . if you had faith even as small as a mustard seed . . . nothing would be impossible" (Matthew 17:20). He healed the boy and sent the demon away.

A mustard seed comes from a mustard plant, which is a tall plant that has pretty yellow flowers. Jesus simply wanted His followers to truly *believe*.

They still doubted Him and doubted that God could do these miracles. If you've struggled with doubts about your faith, this might make you feel better. Those men were sitting *right beside Jesus*, listening to the words He preached, and they still doubted. Sometimes we don't have to have this monumental faith that towers over every aspect of our lives. Many times, we just need enough faith to fill a mustard seed to continue to spark our belief in Jesus.

Are you in a season of having faith like a mountain? Or do you feel like you barely have enough faith to fill a small mustard seed? Jesus says that even just a little faith is a powerful tool for God. God is big enough to shoulder your doubts. You can't ask Him a question that He hasn't heard before. He is ready to provide you with the answers you need. If you are praying for something in your life, do you really *believe* that God can do it? Have faith that God is real and that He has something special to show you in this season of your life.

Jesus, thank You for showing me how to have true faith,
even when it feels like I just have a little.
I want to truly believe in You and have faith
that You'll show up when I need You. Amen.

Jesus Uplifted Women

Then Jesus stood up again and said to the woman, "Where are your accusers? Didn't even one of them condemn you?" "No, Lord," she said. And Jesus said, "Neither do I. Go and sin no more."

JOHN 8:10–11 NLT

Jesus lived in a time period when women were pretty oppressed. They didn't have citizenship. They didn't have rights. They were basically considered property, owned by their fathers and then married off to husbands at a young age. Most women were married off in their early to mid-teenage years. Imagine being told to marry a guy today that you've never even met. It was a hard time for women.

As a respected Jewish teacher, Jesus should not have had much to do with women. But He made a special effort to speak to women, uplift them, and teach them. Jesus came to live and die for the women as much as the men, and He wanted them to know that. There is one particular story in the Bible that shows just how far Jesus was willing to go to protect a woman.

The Pharisees interrupted Jesus during a sermon,

dragging a woman through the crowd to throw her at His feet. She had been caught cheating on her husband. According to Jewish law, they were supposed to stone her to death. The Pharisees wanted to trick Jesus by putting Him in a lose-lose situation. Either He would save the woman or He would uphold the law. Jesus instead simply said, "All right, but let the one who has never sinned throw the first stone!" (John 8:7). That immediately disqualified everyone in the crowd . . . except for Him. Everyone slowly left, leaving Jesus alone with the woman. I can only imagine her terror. She had made the biggest mistake of her life. She was supposed to die right then and there. But this Man stood there, looking down at her, and told her that He didn't condemn her for her bad decisions.

Not only did Jesus save the life of that woman, but He also saved her soul. Women are beautiful creations whom Jesus cares about so very much. He wants to uplift you and show you all that you can be. You should never feel inferior or lesser than. You are *exactly* who God created you to be.

Dear Jesus, thank You for showing the men of Your time that women were worthy of time, attention, and respect. Help me live confidently, knowing that You created me to be exactly the woman I am. Amen.

His Beloved

What marvelous love the Father has extended to us!
Just look at it—we're called children of God!
That's who we really are. But that's also why the world
doesn't recognize us or take us seriously,
because it has no idea who He is or what He's up to.

I JOHN 3:1 THE MESSAGE

The word "beloved" is used many times in the New Testament, but the first time we see it mentioned is when Jesus is baptized by John the Baptist. After Jesus is baptized, the heavens opened, and the Holy Spirit descended in the form of a dove to settle on Jesus. God's voice came from heaven, saying, "This is My beloved Son, with whom I am well-pleased" (Matthew 3:17 CSB). The word "beloved" is translated in the original Greek language to be *agapétos*, which means "to be greatly and divinely loved." It's a derivative of the Greek word *agápē*, which is used to describe the unconditional, no-matter-what kind of love that God has for us. The followers of Jesus began to use the word *agapétos* when referring to one another. Paul often called his church friends *agapétos*, or "my beloved friends." He was reminding them that they were well and truly loved by God and by him.

Jesus has that unbreakable love for you. You are His

beloved daughter. You are loved wholly and perfectly by God. *Agápē* love means that you can't mess it up. It's unconditional, unchanging, unshakeable. God will love you exactly the same amount no matter what you do or where you go in life. You are so important to Him that He sent His own *agapétos* Son to die for you. God's love is so unmeasurable. We see Jesus's love for His disciples. We see His love when He went to the cross for all of us. We see His love when He rose from the dead and kicked sin and death to the curb. You are so, so loved. Even if you feel like you're at your most unlovable right now, God never changes His love for you. Hold tight to that truth: you are His beloved.

God, I don't always understand why You love us, but You do.
Thank You for calling me Your beloved daughter.
Teach me how to show agápē *love to my friends and family.*
Amen.

YOUR MOVE:
Take some time by yourself today. Think about what "beloved" means. Let that truth sink into your heart. Do some journaling about it.

What He Felt

"Father, if You are willing, please take this cup of suffering away from Me. Yet I want Your will to be done, not Mine."

LUKE 22:42 NLT

As we continue to grow in our faith to become more and more like Jesus, it's important to learn about how He handled His emotions. Jesus was 100 percent a human, just like you and me, while also being 100 percent God. He felt deep feelings and tumultuous emotions at times. We can learn from how He handled them.

1. **Jesus was not afraid to feel.** We see Jesus experience a plethora of big feelings. He expressed joy. Sadness. Grief. Anger. Despair. Happiness. Love. Jesus fully embraced His humanity and felt all the feelings that you currently feel right now. And He wasn't afraid to have those feelings. To be human is to have emotions. God created humans in His own image. He created emotions, so we don't have to be ashamed when we are deep in our feelings.

2. **Jesus turned to God with His emotions.** In Luke 22:42, Jesus prayed in the Garden of Gethsemane, beseeching the Father for help because He felt deep despair about the horrific path He was about to walk. Jesus knew the gruesome death awaited Him in a matter of hours. He might have even felt afraid, but He knew that He could talk to God about anything. So, He asked the Father for comfort in His worst moment, and God was there for Him.

You are not defined by the emotions that sweep you away. It's also okay if you have big feelings a lot of the time. Follow in Jesus's footsteps and learn to take those big feels to God for guidance and comfort when they become overwhelming. You were made in God's image, and He made you to have sweeping emotions. But He also made you for relationship with Him. He's ready to help you carry those feelings when they're drowning you. Is there something you need to take to the Lord today?

Jesus, thank You for showing me that it's okay to feel.
Help me learn how to rely on You
when my emotions get too heavy. Amen.

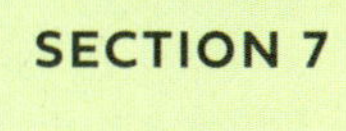

SECTION 7

Against the Tide

"I'm not that kind of king,

not the world's kind of king." –Jesus

JOHN 18:36 THE MESSAGE

Fighting the Current

Therefore, put on every piece of God's armor so you will be able to resist the enemy in the time of evil. Then after the battle you will still be standing firm.

EPHESIANS 6:13 NLT

A red flag on the beach means you shouldn't get in the water. A double red flag on the beach means you *really, really* shouldn't get in the water. But people do anyway, and that's why so many drownings occur on popular beaches every year. Even when the ocean seems harmless, there are hidden dangers. The greatest danger is the riptide. Even in waist-deep water, you can easily lose your footing and get swept out to sea. One moment you're enjoying playing in the waves, and the next moment, you're far from shore and uncertain how to get back.

Swimming against the tide feels impossible when you're caught in a rip current, and that's how it often feels living in today's world. The pressures to conform, to fit in, and to measure up can be overwhelming. Did you know that the best way to escape a riptide is to swim parallel to the coast? Most swimmers panic when they are swept away in a riptide, and they try to swim directly back to shore, fighting the massive current until they tire out. If you swim parallel to the shore, you can escape the rip current and then eventually make your way back to shore. We are called to keep pushing onward in our relationship with Christ, even when we feel like we are getting nowhere. Even when we feel like the current is too strong.

Don't falter. You can do this. Standing on your values is how you build up those spiritual muscles. Don't give up. God is right there alongside you, matching each paddle you make.

God, help me to push against the tide.
I need Your strength to resist the temptation to conform.
It takes so much courage to stay true to who I am in a world
that is constantly changing. But I want to. Amen.

The Monster under the Bed

Trust in the Lord with all your heart;
do not depend on your own understanding.
PROVERBS 3:5 NLT

Some kids have nightmares about monsters under their beds. It's dark down there. You can't see what's hiding. The same could be true about shadows on the wall, things moving around in the closet, creepy dolls or toys in the corner that could come alive at night—some of of these nightmare-inducing fears can last a lifetime. They cause you to lie awake as long as you can, watching for any sign of movement.

Doubt can feel like a monster under the bed. It's there. You know it's there, and you don't want it to come out and raise its ugly head. We all have doubts about our faith from time to time. Anyone who says they have never questioned their faith doesn't have a deep one. Wrestling with doubts is how we grow. For centuries, people have wrestled with doubts about Jesus and who He said He was. Christians have wondered if God is really real. Even pastors have walked away from their beliefs due to doubt at times. And yet, even after centuries of people having doubts, our faith is still the strongest in the world. That's because God is bigger and stronger than our doubts.

Sometimes it can seem as if we're fighting an uphill battle against our own minds. It's okay to ask questions and seek answers. God is big enough to handle your questions. Truth stands up against doubt every time. So, ask your questions, do research, and talk to trusted church leaders. Don't be afraid of that monster under the bed or shadows on the ceiling. Turns out, it might just be someone trying to keep you distracted and fearful to keep you quiet.

Jesus, sometimes I do have doubts about You and my faith.
I don't want to have them, but there are questions in my mind.
Help me find the right answers so I can
walk forward with confidence. Amen.

YOUR MOVE:
Write down three questions you have about your faith. Take them to a pastor or a trusted church leader and talk through them this week.

False Realities

Those who trust God's action in them find that God's Spirit is in them—living and breathing God! Obsession with self in these matters is a dead end; attention to God leads us out into the open, into a spacious, free life. Focusing on the self is the opposite of focusing on God.

ROMANS 8:5-8 THE MESSAGE

You're scrolling through your feed, looking at pictures from your friends and kids in your town. One after another . . . fun places, smiling people, clear skin, beautiful makeup . . . perfect. They all have perfect lives. They have that "sparkle" that you don't have. They have the best family, and you don't. Those kids get to travel to fun places, and you're stuck at home. Compared to their lives, your life is so *boring*.

Influencers tell you to buy this makeup or wear your hair in that hairstyle. They give you book reviews, movie reviews, food reviews. They tell you what's good for you. They tell you what's bad for you. And we listen to each and every word that they say. If they demonstrate something to you, it must be real, right?

Welcome to the world of social media. The world of curated realities. There's often a strategy behind everything you see online, with many posts carefully crafted to highlight the best moments. While it may seem like everyone is living a picture-perfect life, remember that behind the polished images, there are real stories and experiences, often enhanced with photo editing and filters. Influencers, too, are just everyday people navigating their own journeys. They face challenges and insecurities, just like anyone else.

The world of social media is not actual reality—there are algorithms to keep you scrolling, curated content to lead you to buy something, and false storylines that make you feel less than. That's why it's important to approach it with a balanced perspective, recognizing both the creativity and the humanity behind each post. Maybe it's time to put down your phone. Go outside. Enjoy the gorgeous world around you—rest assured that it is real. And it's so much better than the false realities people dwell in on social media platforms.

God, I don't want to believe the lies planted by social media. People work so hard to paint themselves in the perfect light. But You made me just the way that I am. Thank You. Amen.

Be Careful, Little Eyes

"Your eye is like a lamp that provides light for your body. When your eye is healthy, your whole body is filled with light. But when your eye is unhealthy, your whole body is filled with darkness. And if the light you think you have is actually darkness, how deep that darkness is!"

MATTHEW 6:22–23 NLT

There was a children's song you may have sung in Sunday school. It goes, "Oh, be careful little eyes what you see; oh, be careful little eyes what you see; for the Father up above is looking down in love; oh, be careful little eyes what you see." It's a simple tune, but the song has an important message. The Bible has multiple verses about being careful about what we listen to or look at.

Jesus taught His followers that "your eye is like a lamp that provides light for your body . . . when your eye is unhealthy, your whole body is filled with darkness." What do you think Jesus is telling us here?

It's so easy for darkness to enter our souls through our eyes. What we watch, what we look at, and what we read is important. Are you keeping your eyes healthy by only focusing them on good and honorable things? Or are you filling your soul with inappropriate images, endless social media scrolling, and movies and shows that don't honor God?

Pray and ask the Lord to show you the areas in your life that are allowing sin to enter. Maybe you need to take a break from social media. Maybe the Holy Spirit is convicting you of something you're looking at on your phone. Or maybe you're not watching shows that are pure and good.

Jesus tells His followers in another passage, "And if your eye causes you to sin, gouge it out and throw it away" (Matthew 18:9). Jesus means that we sometimes need to forcefully remove the negative influences from our path. Take a break from social media. Watch something else on TV. Listen to what the Holy Spirit might be asking you to do. And do it.

Jesus, show me areas in my life where I can cultivate healthier choices through what I see. Help me to embrace positive influences so I can grow closer to You. Amen.

Constant Connectivity

The Lord is my shepherd; I have all that I need.
He lets me rest in green meadows; He leads me beside peaceful streams. He renews my strength. He guides me along right paths, bringing honor to His name.

PSALM 23:1–3 NLT

Take a quick moment and grab your phone.

You didn't have to move far, did you? Your phone was probably sitting right beside you as you sat to read this book. You probably had it face up so you would see if you received any notifications. Perhaps you haven't been able to finish very many sentences in this book without glancing at it.

We live in a culture of constant connectivity. We never have to be disconnected from our society, our friends, or anyone. Our phones transport us into a world of networks and instant relationships. We can talk to whomever we want, right now. It's never been easier to keep up with friends, talk to people, and stay on top of current news and trends.

But the constant connectivity that we live for on our phones can create a deep soul-disconnect from God and true relationships. It's been said that many people today are feeling more lonely and isolated than ever before. Even scientists are studying the potential harm that social media can do to present-day teenagers.[1] Some teens are struggling with real-life interactions, often hiding behind their digital personas and distancing their true selves from others. We might be more disconnected from one another—and even from God—than in previous generations, all while being constantly plugged in to the little screens we hold in our hands.

If the thought of going a day without your phone fills you with terror, you might need to ponder whether you're too entwined with your screen. Do you focus on God during your time with Him? Or do you constantly glance at your phone to make sure you're still connected to anyone who might need you? What would "disconnecting" look like for you? What if you turned your phone off for quiet time every morning for a week? What if you focused on spending real time with people instead of digital time?

God, my life has become entwined with my phone.
I have so much trouble setting aside my constant connectivity.
But nothing compares to my true soul-connection with You
and others. Help me to disconnect from that false world
and connect back to You. Amen.

1 The Dark Side of Social Media: A new study finds spending less time on social media leads to greater well-being. (https://www.psychologytoday.com/us/blog/no-more-fomo/202406/the-dark-side-of-social-media) June 21, 2024 by Gary Goldfield, Ph.D.

Just a Taste

"You won't die!" the serpent replied to the woman. "God knows that your eyes will be opened as soon as you eat it, and you will be like God, knowing both good and evil."

GENESIS 3:4–5 NLT

Let's be real. We give Eve a pretty bad rap. I mean, she kind of destroyed the entire world with one bad decision, right?

Actually, Eve wasn't alone in her bad decision. In fact, Adam was literally standing right next to her, not saying a thing while the serpent convinced her to take a bite. Eve's sin was control. Adam's sin was apathy. And here we are today, living in a broken world.

It's easy to blame Adam and Eve for our current situation, but they are no different from us. When we are tempted to do something we know we shouldn't, it's exactly like that silver-tongued serpent, whispering in our ear:

It's not that bad. You could be doing so many worse things. Your friend is doing it, and she isn't a bad person. You won't be a bad person either. It's no big deal. It's a small thing. No one will ever know.

Just a taste. That's all Eve wanted. Just a small bite to see what the fuss was about. Adam wasn't stopping her. Maybe it wasn't that big of a deal.

Temptation is not the sin. Giving in to temptation is. If Eve had just walked away, things would have been different. If Adam had had the courage to step up and tell Eve that it wasn't the right thing to do, we wouldn't be where we are. But they gave in . . . just a little . . . and we do it every day.

What are the temptations that whisper in your ear? Take a look around. There might be serpents in your life disguised as friends, working to convince you to make one small bad decision. But that one bad decision can lead to life-changing consequences.

God, I need Your help to face the whispering serpent when it comes. Show me the temptations in my own life and give me the strength to walk away. Amen.

YOUR MOVE:

Take a moment and think about the last time you gave in to temptation. What were the signs? Can you identity that small whisper that pulled you in? Think about how to walk away the next time temptation comes.

Pushing against Hate

Hatred starts fights, but love pulls a quilt over the bickering.

PROVERBS 10:12 THE MESSAGE

It's easy to become entangled in disagreements, especially with differing opinions clashing all around us—on social media, in the news, and on college campuses. While engaging in dialogue and fostering important discussions can be valuable, it often takes a turn for the worse, quickly devolving into name-calling and hostility. Hatred is never a path to peace; it only leads to anger, arguments, and conflict, sometimes escalating to larger struggles. Instead, we have the opportunity to choose understanding and compassion as a way forward.

We are never called to hatred. No matter what a person believes, says, or does toward us, hatred is *never* the answer. Don't get sucked in by arguments or fights on social media, and never solely rely on what others say online to dictate your beliefs about a subject. If you sense hatred behind someone's words or actions, then that isn't coming from God, and we need to tread carefully.

Jesus tells His disciples, "Your love for one another will prove to the world that you are My disciples" (John 13:35 NLT). Our *love* will define us. Our love. Not our political beliefs. Not our race. Not our wealth. Not the social justice movements we subscribe to. Our love. Love does not discriminate. Love does not judge. Love is a lifestyle.

My dear friend, the only way our world will change is if we show it what God's love looks like. Be the change this world needs. Your love could be the catalyst for God to do a new work in your community.

Jesus, I want to spread the love that You have for me to everyone else. Show me how to fight hate with Your amazing love. Amen.

Rejection to Resilience

"If the world hates you, keep in mind that it hated Me first. If you belonged to the world, it would love you as its own. As it is, you do not belong to the world, but I have chosen you out of the world. That is why the world hates you. Remember what I told you: 'A servant is not greater than his master.' If they persecuted Me, they will persecute you also. If they obeyed My teaching, they will obey yours also. They will treat you this way because of My name, for they do not know the one who sent Me."

JOHN 15:18–21 NIV

Rejection can feel like a heavy weight, can't it? Whether it's not being picked for a team, feeling left out of a group, or even facing criticism, it's easy to feel down when things don't go our way. But let's take a look at what Jesus says in John 15 (above). He reminds us that rejection is part of the journey of following Him. Just as He faced rejection, we will too, but that doesn't have to define us. Instead of letting these experiences pull us down, we can transform them into resilience.

How, you ask? It could be a simple change in mindset. Instead of viewing rejection as a failure, see it as an opportunity to grow. Ask yourself: *What can I learn from this?* Each experience, even the painful ones, can teach you valuable lessons and help you develop resilience. Remember, it's okay to feel weak or hurt. Don't brush your feelings aside. Acknowledging them is the first step toward healing. It's in those moments that you can talk to God about your feelings and grow closer to Him. It's in those moments that you experience His deep love, His compassion, and His heart for you. It's in those moments that you learn it's not all up to you, but that you can draw on God's strength and wisdom to keep going, to make your next right step.

Rejection is not the end of your story, but a new chapter of growth. You have the strength to rise, learn, and shine! Keep being the incredible person God created you to be—you'll see this time in a new light in a few years. Give it time, give it to God, and let Him draw you close through this.

Dear Lord, when I feel rejected,
guide me to see it as an opportunity for growth.
Teach me to lean on You for comfort and wisdom.
Fill me with Your peace and remind me that
I am never truly alone. In Jesus's name, amen.

Not Cool Enough

"What blessings await you when people hate you and exclude you and mock you and curse you as evil because you follow the Son of Man."

LUKE 6:22 NLT

What are you willing to put aside to follow Jesus? What if God asked you to step away from popularity? What if following Jesus took you from being well-liked and cool to being outcast and ignored?

Everyone wants to belong. The desire can feel overwhelming. When we're kids, we don't care what other people think *at all*. We had no problems screaming and running and getting dirty without a moment's hesitation.

Today, on the other hand, you may feel a little more self-conscious at times. You might feel caught in between—no longer enjoying the carefree days of childhood, yet not able to change your circumstances as quickly as adults do. Do you feel as if you belong today? If not, how strong is your desire to belong? Is it a *desperate need*? Do you want to belong so badly that you are allowing this desire to overshadow your joy and authenticity?

We may think that if we just act a certain way or dress in a specific style, we'll finally find acceptance. But here's the question—will you be happy if you are not living as your authentic self? If you are pretending to be something other than what God made you to be? Is there any joy found in that? When you stop trying to be someone you're not, you create space for genuine joy. Authenticity attracts the right people into your life and allows you to experience deeper connections. Remember, joy is found when you align your life with who God created you to be.

Dear Lord, thank You for creating me as Your masterpiece. Help me to embrace my uniqueness and to find joy in being my authentic self. When I feel the pressure to fit in, remind me of Your love and acceptance. Surround me with friends who celebrate who I am, and give me the confidence to shine brightly for You. In Jesus's name, amen.

Hold Steady

My dear, dear friends! I love you so much.
I do want the very best for you.
You make me feel such joy, fill me with such pride.
Don't waver. Stay on track, steady in God.

PHILIPPIANS 4:1 THE MESSAGE

Imagine being on a giant ship in the 1700s. You're out on the deck in the middle of a big storm. Sailors are running everywhere, securing the sails and rigging. Monster waves rise up on both sides. It's a sailor's worst nightmare, being caught out at sea in the midst of so much raw power. The crew begins to lose hope.

Then the captain bellows over the crashing waves, raising his voice to be heard, "Hold her steady!"

The helmsman at the wheel braces himself and uses all his strength to hold the boat's course steady and true. The captain remembers what many of the crew have forgotten: sometimes the only way forward is through.

That sailor's phrase, "hold steady," is still used today. It's a reminder to stay the course no matter how difficult the circumstances are. Standing against the tides of this world is like taking a ship right through a storm. You will be tossed from side to side by mighty waves of doubt and opposition. But God, the patient

Captain, is constantly reminding you, lifting His voice over the sounds of the storm, "Hold steady!"

You're the helmsman at the wheel of the ship. It's so, so hard to fight against the current, the waves, and the tides. But you can beat it. You can keep heading forward, no matter what comes your way. The helmsman isn't in charge of setting the heading. That's the captain's job. The helmsman simply obeys the captain's order and keeps the ship going in that direction. Jesus has set our heading. He is leading us into a life of joy, blessings, and fulfillment. It doesn't mean the way is easy, but it's the absolute best way to reach our final, eternal destination. Don't give up! Hold steady. Stay the course. God is so incredibly proud of you.

God, the waves of this world are overwhelming me.
Show me the heading. Tell me where to go in my life.
I need You to help me walk forward today. Amen.

YOUR MOVE:

Take some time to sit and listen for what God may have to tell you today. We get so busy, sometimes we forget to listen for the captain's heading.

SECTION 8

Finding Your Purpose

For everything, absolutely everything,
above and below, visible and invisible,
rank after rank after rank of angels—
everything got started in Him
and finds its purpose in Him.

COLOSSIANS 1:16 THE MESSAGE

Created for a Purpose

"You can make many plans,
but the Lord's purpose will prevail."
PROVERBS 19:21 NLT

There are over eight billion people in the world right now. Somehow God knows each and every one of those people backward and forward. He knows them, and He loves them. For each and every life that is born every day, God has a specific purpose and plan for that individual. We don't always understand God's purposes and plans, but we can trust that He does *have* a plan.

The day you were born . . . the day you took your first breath, God was right there. There is an important reason that you're here on this planet right now. God has something specific in mind for your life that only you can do. It may be something big and public, like being a politician, or it could be something more behind-the-scenes, like being a mom to wonderful children. Maybe God's purpose for your life is to have you travel across the world as a missionary. And maybe it's to have you stay right where you are and be a missionary there. Every single person's purpose is unique, and only you can fulfill God's plan for you.

Our lives are so much more than going through the motions: going to school, doing homework, or messaging our friends. There is deep meaning to living, and if we ask God, He will show us what that deeper purpose is. So many people live solely for the betterment of themselves. Their only purpose is to do anything and everything to be happy. But they are missing out on true fulfillment. True fulfillment isn't the clothes that we wear, or the friends that we have, or whom we date. True happiness and joy come from understanding God's plans for us and living them out to their fullest.

You are a very special daughter of God. He brought you to this world for a reason. There are people out there waiting for you to love them, interact with them, and offer them hope. God's purpose for you may initially look different than what you had planned for yourself, but it's always immensely better. Start asking God what His purpose is for you. He will start showing you why you're so incredibly special to Him.

God, I pray that You will show me Your true purpose for my life.
I want to live out Your plans for me and not my own.
Help me to impact the people around me. Amen.

Superpower

Do not be conformed to this age, but be transformed by the renewing of your mind, so that you may discern what is the good, pleasing, and perfect will of God.

ROMANS 12:2 CSB

Let's say you have the option to gain one superpower in life. What would it be? Maybe flying like Superman. Or teleporting or mind reading. Think about it until you have that one perfect superpower in mind.

Superpowers would allow us to do something that we can't do on our own. Superheroes are extraordinary because of their powers, and that's why their stories are so popular. People wish for the power to be something greater than they are. Who wouldn't want to be faster, stronger, or better in some way?

When we become Christians, God grants us some of His power. He gifts us with spiritual gifts, and He asks us to follow in His footsteps and use these powers in the way He shows us to. One particular superpower we can all have with a bit of work is discernment. Charles Spurgeon, an influential preacher in the 1800s, said, "Discernment is not knowing the difference between right and wrong. It is knowing the difference between right and almost right."

Having discernment means that you can step back and analyze a situation and determine quickly the best and truest path of action to take. It can also help you see past another person's walls and look into their hearts. Discernment is an amazing superpower. It will help you to stay out of trouble . . . to make the best decisions . . . and to care deeply for others. How do you get discernment? Romans 12:2 says, "Be transformed by the renewing of your mind, so that you may discern what is the good, pleasing, and perfect will of God." To grow in discernment, you need to clear out some space in your mind for God to work. Spend time with Him. Learn from Him. Pray to Him when you face hard choices and ask Him to show you the correct path. Discernment is a gift that will never fail you. It is the superpower that will make you the best version of yourself.

Jesus, I want the gift of discernment in my life.
I invite You into my mind to renew my thoughts
so I can clear the clutter.
Show me how to discern well today. Amen.

Up Ahead

Yes, indeed—God is my salvation.
I trust, I won't be afraid. God—yes God!—
is my strength and song, best of all, my salvation!

ISAIAH 12:2 THE MESSAGE

My family did a lot of road-tripping when I was growing up. Flying with a family of five wasn't financially possible. So we all loaded up into our family Suburban and explored various parts of the United States. On one particular road trip, my family drove from Texas to California, and we often found ourselves in rather perilous circumstances. While we were driving across New Mexico, a blizzard appeared out of the blue. There were no towns around us, only the road stretching ahead and behind. What started as a light snowfall (which was super-cool to some Texans) quickly became a fast-blowing whiteout blizzard. We could not see the car in front of us. We could barely see the edge of the road. It was terrifying because we had absolutely no visibility of the road ahead.

Looking ahead to the future can feel like staring into a whiteout blizzard. You have no idea what the years ahead will look like, and your life is going to change quite a bit once you become an adult. It's totally normal to be afraid of what is coming. In fact, fearing the unknown is pretty much commonplace these days. But the truth is, we cannot do one single thing about it. Staring ahead at that whiteout blizzard won't make it clear. All we can do is slow down to a crawl and creep forward an inch at a time, trusting God to take us forward.

You are never going to have to face something alone. Whether you're terrified of going to college or scared about what job you might get or worried about where you will live, those big changes don't have to be navigated by yourself. You have the most powerful Being in the universe, God, standing by you. He walked with you through the hard times in your past, and He's going to walk with you through them in the future. You don't have to be scared of the blizzard. You have the best Guide right next to you.

God, I get so scared of what my life will look like.
I wish I knew what was coming.
But You are with me, no matter what.
Help me to trust in Your strength. Amen.

Giftings

There are different kinds of spiritual gifts,
but the same Spirit is the source of them all.
There are different kinds of service,
but we serve the same Lord. God works in different ways,
but it is the same God who does the work in all of us.

1 CORINTHIANS 12:4–6 NLT

God created you for a specific reason, and He gave you some amazing gifts that will allow you to accomplish those purposes. When we become Christians, the Holy Spirit comes to live in our hearts, which is a really profound act that is hard to grasp sometimes. The Holy Spirit sources us with spiritual gifts that allow us to serve ourselves, other Christians, and other people. First Corinthians 12 and Ephesians 4:11–16 are passages in the Bible that talk more in-depth about spiritual gifts. We all have a gift, and yours might look very different from another's.

Examples of spiritual gifts include teaching, serving, encouraging, giving, leading, discernment, extending mercy, and helping, to name a few. If you feel like God might be putting a spark in your heart for ministry, your spiritual gift might be teaching, serving, or leading. If you love telling other people about the hope that you have found in Jesus, your gift might be evangelizing, which means sharing what you believe. If people often come to you for advice in hard circumstances, you could be gifted in discernment or words of wisdom. When you become a member of God's family, you absolutely *will* have a gift, even if it takes some time for it to develop and for you to grow in it.

No one's gifts are "better" than others'. Some people have gifts that allow them to pay attention to how others are feeling, what they aren't saying, and how they can speak to what's really going on in their hearts. Whatever your gifts are, use them for God. They will help make you into the woman warrior you are meant to be.

God, I want to learn what my spiritual gifts are.
Show me the ways You have gifted me to serve You. Amen.

YOUR MOVE:

Read I Corinthians 12 and Ephesians 4:11–16 and start exploring which gifts might be yours.

To Love and to Cherish

For we are God's masterpiece.
He has created us anew in Christ Jesus,
so we can do the good things He planned for us long ago.

EPHESIANS 2:10 NLT

I will never forget the moment I stood in front of a crowd of people and stated my marriage vows to my husband, Nathan. A part of the vows go something like "for richer, for poorer . . . in sickness and in health . . . to love and to cherish . . . as long as we both shall live." I had been waiting for many years to meet a man who would truly love and cherish me. During my high-school and early adulthood years, I had been on a few first dates and there were many crushes I had that were never returned. But I never had a boyfriend, not until I was in my mid-twenties, when I met Nathan. I'm so glad God never planned for me to date anyone else before him, because I was constantly looking for a man to *cherish* me and love me.

So many young women are looking for the same thing. We have an empty place in our hearts that we think can only be filled with a relationship that makes us feel wanted. But we never learn how to truly cherish ourselves. Do you realize how amazing you are? Ephesians 2:10 says, "For we are God's masterpiece." That's you! You're a true work of art. You're talented. Gifted. Special. Beautiful. And made exactly right.

I wasn't ready to meet my husband until I had truly learned what it meant to love and to cherish myself before looking for that from a man. That's not easy to do. That little empty place in your heart can't be filled by a boy. It can only be filled with a surety and confidence that comes from God. Insecurity shrinks when we realize just how amazing God made us. God may bring your greatest true love into your life someday, and that's wonderful. Nathan is my soul mate, and I adore him. But he doesn't complete me. And when he cherishes me, I can recognize it because I've learned to cherish myself. I know that I'm God's daughter. And that's the best title I'll ever have.

God, thank You for making me just the way that I am.
Thank You for crafting me to be a masterpiece.
Help me learn how to cherish myself. Amen.

God's Dreams

"May Your Kingdom come soon.
May Your will be done on earth, as it is in heaven."

MATTHEW 6:10 NLT

Children's animated movies speak of when "dreams come true" and "when you wish upon a star." We are taught in grade school to dream big and imagine all the places we can go in our lives. Many adults will tell us to chase after our dreams. You probably have dreams of the future as well. Hopes, goals, aspirations . . . they are all out there for you, and you want to make your dreams a reality someday.

But what about God's dreams? Remember how we've been talking about finding our purpose? Many of us already think we have figured out our purpose, and that's to follow our personal dreams and goals. But have you asked God if His dreams align with yours? I think you'll find that they oftentimes do because God made you to have big dreams, but there are times when God might have different dreams for your future.

As you explore your aspirations, take a moment to seek God's guidance in your journey. Pray for clarity and openness to His will, allowing space for His dreams to unfold in your life. Remember that God's plans for you are rooted in love and a deep understanding of who you are. While you may feel certain that you're on the right path, there may be times when God gently redirects you, leading you toward new opportunities and experiences that you hadn't considered. Embrace the possibility that His dreams may lead you to unexpected but incredible places.

You can trust God with your dreams. Hold them with open hands and allow Him to write His own story with your life. It may have its ups and downs, but God is the greatest Storyteller of them all.

God, part of me is afraid to give my dreams over to You.
I ask that You hold them close.
Show me what Your dreams are for my life.
I want to follow Your plan for my life. Amen.

Singleness and Marriage

So I say to those who aren't married and to widows—
it's better to stay unmarried, just as I am.

1 CORINTHIANS 7:8 NLT

Maybe you don't have any desire for marriage or a family. You know what? That is perfectly okay. The apostle Paul never married. In fact, he told the church at Corinth that "it's better to stay unmarried, just as I am," because then you can give your full attention to God. There is a deep blessing in being single.

In this season of your life, you have a unique opportunity to explore your passions, invest in relationships, and grow in your faith without the distractions that often come with romantic commitments. Embrace this time as a chance to discover who you are and what God has called you to do. You can pour energy into your dreams, serve in your community, and develop deep friendships that enrich your life. Remember, being single does not mean you are incomplete. It may just mean you have the freedom and time to do what you are called to be doing during this season of your life—to cultivate a vibrant relationship with God and to impact the world in meaningful ways.

So celebrate this season of your life! Trust that God has a purpose for you, whether it includes marriage in the future or not. Focus on seeking Him first. You are valuable, whole, and loved just as you are.

God, You have a plan for my life,
whether it's to be single, dating, or married.
Help me to protect my heart so I can be ready
for the future You're planning for me. Amen.

Working Diligently

Work willingly at whatever you do,
as though you were working for the Lord
rather than for people.
Remember that the Lord will give you
an inheritance as your reward,
and that the Master you are serving is Christ.

COLOSSIANS 3:23–24 NLT

There's a pretty high likelihood that you're going to have a job someday. We all need to make a living somehow, and the unfortunate part of growing up means the added responsibility of paying for rent, buying food, paying for insurance, etc. Work is a part of life, but it also opens the door to personal growth and discovering your passions. Many people may find it challenging to work five days a week, but by shifting our perspective, we can see work as a chance to contribute, learn, and connect with others. So, how can we embrace this journey and view work in a more positive light as we move forward?

When we work for God's sake and not for ours, it becomes an act of worship instead of something we have to do to get by. Paul tells the church at Corinth to "work willingly at whatever you do, as though you were working for the Lord rather than for people." When we get up in the morning and get ready for school or work, everything becomes a little brighter when we remind ourselves that we are working for God and not for ourselves. That means no matter what happens during the day, it's all okay in the end because it wasn't for you anyway.

If you're paralyzed by the prospect of choosing a career for yourself someday, let some of the pressure fall away. If you work willingly at whatever you do for God's glory and sake instead of your own, you're going to be honoring Him and making Him proud. The heart behind your work is what matters more than anything to God. Whether you're working behind a cash register, behind a desk, behind the wheel of a truck, or behind a stroller . . . God will use you someday. All you have to do is put your hands to work and set your heart on God.

Dear God, I want to learn to work diligently
for Your glory and not for mine.
Whatever I do with my life, I want to do it for You. Amen.

A New Kind of Fishing

Walking along the beach of Lake Galilee, Jesus saw two brothers: Simon (later called Peter) and Andrew. They were fishing, throwing their nets into the lake. It was their regular work. Jesus said to them, "Come with Me. I'll make a new kind of fisherman out of you. I'll show you how to catch men and women instead of perch and bass." They didn't ask questions, but simply dropped their nets and followed.

MATTHEW 4:18-20 THE MESSAGE

There is one purpose in life that is the same for all Christians, and that's our mission to tell other people about Jesus and what He has done in our lives. It's the biggest purpose that we'll ever pursue, no matter where we go in our futures.

The disciples were just regular people. They weren't heroes. They weren't wealthy or influential. A few of them were fishermen who had to work hard to make their meager living. Peter and Andrew were out fishing one day, pursuing their life's purpose, making a living, when everything changed in an instant. Jesus called out to them and said, "Come with Me. I'll make a new kind of fisherman out of you." Something in their hearts must have changed the moment He spoke, because they immediately rowed to shore, dropped their nets, and followed Jesus for the rest of their lives. The purpose they had picked out for themselves was suddenly forgotten. The new purpose that Jesus had set before them was all they could do now.

God's purpose will always outshine our own plans. Jesus is asking each of us to lay aside our own checklists and take up His calling: to share His story with the world. It's the most fulfilling and the most rewarding goal one could ever have. If we are chasing after that purpose, we'll always be pointing in the right direction. Jesus wants you to practice a new kind of fishing in your community. Are you ready to grab a net?

Jesus, Your purposes for my life far outshine anything I could come up with. Peter and Andrew never regretted leaving their nets that day. Teach me how to fish for people's souls. Amen.

YOUR MOVE:
Think of one person in your life who might need to hear the story of Jesus. How might you go about talking to them about what Jesus has done for you?

Turning Off Distractions

So I say, let the Holy Spirit guide your lives. Then you won't be doing what your sinful nature craves. The sinful nature wants to do evil, which is just the opposite of what the Spirit wants. And the Spirit gives us desires that are the opposite of what the sinful nature desires. These two forces are constantly fighting each other, so you are not free to carry out your good intentions.

GALATIANS 5:16–17 NLT

Imagine you're in a big room that's filled with obstacles like chairs, desks, and boxes. Your mission is to walk from one side of the room to the other. No problem, right? Except now imagine that you're blindfolded. It's going to be a bit of a stumble to get from one side of the room to the other, and you'll get a lot of bumps and bruises on the way. Now, imagine that someone is standing on the other side of the room, giving you orders about where to walk and when to step over something. That person is your guide. Your compass. They will help you navigate through the obstacles of the room. For the last exercise, imagine that the entire room is filled with a crowd of people, all shouting, talking, and singing at the top of their lungs. You're blindfolded and wandering around, trying desperately to hear the voice of your guide at the other end. Are you going to be able to find your way with all that racket? Not easily.

Oftentimes, we grumble something like, "If only God would just *tell* me what to do. He never does." Finding our life's purpose feels aimless, like stumbling through a huge room blindfolded. But what if God *is* trying to lead us through the chaos? What if we simply can't hear Him because of life's distractions yelling for our attention?

In today's world, you are bombarded with distractions all vying for your focus. Snapping, messaging, photo-taking, scrolling, making shareable content, watching shows, following influencers . . . wow. It's really loud. And really exhausting. What if you turned it all off for a bit? Silence is the best environment for listening.

God, I forget how loud life's distractions can be.
I'm going to silence the noise so I can listen to You. Amen.

YOUR MOVE:

Think about what you could do to silence the noise. Do you need to take a break from social media for a while? Do you need to set your own boundaries on screen time? What is distracting you each day?

SECTION 9

Resilient Hope

So roll up your sleeves,
get your head in the game,
be totally ready to receive the gift
that's coming when Jesus arrives.

I PETER 1:13 THE MESSAGE

A Life of Hope

But those who trust in the LORD will find new strength.
They will soar high on wings like eagles.
They will run and not grow weary.
They will walk and not faint.

ISAIAH 40:31 NLT

The last section of this book is titled, "Resilient Hope." I hope that by the end of this devotional, you'll truly understand what that means and why our faith is the only one in the world like it.

The world feels pretty hopeless sometimes. So what does it mean to have a life full of hope? Hope and trust go hand in hand. Hope is the emotional and spiritual mindset that we get when we learn to fully trust. Having hope comes *after* the action of trusting the Lord.

Even when it feels as if our lives are falling to pieces, we can have hope in the future *because* we trust that the Lord is in control. So many people are afraid of death, but we have hope in life after death *because* we trust that what the Bible says is true.

Many of your friends may feel like their lives are hopeless and that things will never improve for them. But we can live with a hope in our hearts for tomorrow *because* we trust that God will walk ahead of us the entire way, leading us onward.

My grandmother passed away a few years ago. She was a spiritual mentor to me, and she fought cancer for four years. One of the verses I remember her repeating was Isaiah 40:31. It's become a very special verse to me. The prophet Isaiah writes, "But those who trust in the Lord will find new strength. They will soar high on wings like eagles. They will run and not grow weary. They will walk and not faint." The strength to endure the trials of life comes from trusting that God will not abandon you. My grandmother walked forward with more courage than I've ever seen, and it's because she trusted the Lord with her future. Do you need some hope in your life? Are your trust muscles strong? Or do they need a bit of a workout?

God, trusting You is so hard to do.
But I want to have hope for the future,
so I put my fears in Your hands,
and I trust that You'll lead me onward in Your plan. Amen.

Resiliency

Therefore, my dear brothers and sisters,
be steadfast, immovable, always excelling
in the Lord's work, because you know
that your labor in the Lord is not in vain.

I CORINTHIANS 15:58 CSB

Let's talk about being *resilient*. It's a word that you might get hung up on, but it's so rich in its meaning. Resiliency means that you can adjust to the circumstances that come to you in your life. If you were a champion boxer in the ring, you wouldn't let any punch keep you down. You'd just keep getting back up over and over again. That's resiliency.

Resiliency does not come naturally for everyone. Some of us can be thrown off by the smallest things, and we can make the little bits of chaos feel like monster thunderstorms. However, resilient people are steadfast. They aren't going to give up, and they are going to keep standing back up when they get knocked down. No matter what you throw at them, they aren't fazed. They are confident. Self-assured. Unflappable.

You know the telltale sign of people with resiliency? They have a strong, unwavering trust in God. They can get back up because they know that there's something to get back up for. Resilient people can adjust to life's many changing circumstances because they trust that God is the constant, even in chaos. Resilient people can let go of the little things because they know that they have bigger, God-sized plans ahead of them.

Doesn't that sound like the person you want to become? You can start right now. Grow in your personal grit. Stick to your beliefs and your faith no matter what the world throws at you. Be the kind of person who just keeps getting back up when the world tries to take you down. You are meant to be a warrior for the Lord. Warriors never give up the fight.

God, I'm Your warrior. Life will deliver hits and punches,
but You give me the strength to keep fighting.
Thank You for teaching me how to be steadfast,
no matter what. Amen.

The Wonder of Our Faith

There's no one quite like You among the gods, O Lord,
and nothing to compare with Your works.
All the nations You made are on their way,
ready to give honor to You, O Lord,
ready to put Your beauty on display,
parading Your greatness, and the great things You do—
God, You're the one, there's no one but You!

PSALM 86:8-10 THE MESSAGE

Wow.

When was the last time you looked at something awe-inspiring and just said . . . wow? Mountains often produce that response. Sometimes, the vastness of the ocean will make us stand in absolute wonder. Or the canopy of stars painting the night sky. There are so many amazing, beautiful, striking scenes in this world that take our breath away. And that emotion, that feeling, that should be the wonder that our faith wakes up in us. Our God is the Creator of all of those beautiful, awe-inspiring scenes we just talked about. He is the Painter who dreamed up the sunrise, who imagined the mountains, and who breathed the stars into being. And the truth that's even more wonderful?

He loves us. And we get to have a relationship with the same God who paints the sky above us.

The awe and wonder is so easy to forget. We get busy with our daily lives and everything we have to do. We don't even glance up at the beautiful world we live in. And we so often forget its Creator. But that incredible Being who crafted this planet also crafted you, and you're so special to Him. That should never get old! It's absolutely incredible!

Psalm 86:10 says, "God, You're the one, there's no one but You!" God is singular. Nothing compares to Him because He is above it all. He is supreme. Grand. Filled with splendor. We can't wrap our minds around His greatness. But what we can do is sit in absolute wonder at the beauty of our faith.

God . . . wow! Amen.

YOUR MOVE:

As you go about your day, find a few wonderful things that draw your attention and make you go, "wow!" Say a quick prayer of thanks to God for that thing.

Glimmers

You love Him even though you have never seen Him.
Though you do not see Him now, you trust Him;
and you rejoice with a glorious, inexpressible joy.
The reward for trusting Him will be the salvation of your souls.

I PETER 1:8–9 NLT

You have probably heard faith stories from people that are a bit shocking. Maybe you heard a story of someone on drugs who found Jesus and changed. You might have heard the testimony of a Muslim terrorist who had a dream about Jesus and became a Christian. Maybe your pastor told you faith stories that were grand, amazing, and shocking. It's true that God can work in big ways, and He still does miracles and major life transformation all the time.

But God moves in the little things in life too. Yes, God shows up in everyday life just like He has shown up in big ways. There are little glimmers of Jesus everywhere. He's in the joy-filled laughter of the kids at the park. He's in the smile of a stranger at the grocery store. He's there when you're with your friends, and in algebra class. He's there when you're stressed and busy and someone stops and tells you something encouraging. He's there.

Just like glimmers reflecting off a shimmering stream, little joy-filled moments in our lives reflect Jesus's love and care for us. God can be found in the quiet, mundane tasks of living even as He can be found in miracles in the past and present. Your story is your story, and God has moved in your life just as much as He moved in the life of a terrorist. They just have different shapes in the glimmer. There are beautiful moments that remind us of who God is. I think God loves to be in the tiny details to remind us that He cares about even the smallest thing. He's trying to get your attention with those sweet glimmers. Are you watching for them?

Jesus, what are You trying to speak to me?
I want to pay attention to where You show up today.
I'll keep my eyes open for Your joy-filled glimmers of hope.
Thank You for caring about me. Amen.

Unshakable

Those who trust in the LORD are like Mount Zion.
It cannot be shaken; it remains forever.

PSALM 125:1 CSB

Let's talk about being unshakable. Psalm 125:1 states, "Those who trust in the LORD are like Mount Zion. It cannot be shaken; it remains forever." There's that word again: *trust*. Becoming unshakable in your faith starts with that small word with such big implications. God wants us to trust Him. When the doubts come about what we believe, our trust muscles will be so strong that we are able to turn those doubts away and continue to trust in what God has already told us. When other students in our schools and communities pepper us with questions about our faith, we'll be able to trust that God is who He says He is, no matter the questions. Being unshakable is like being a mountain. Have you ever seen a mountain shrink away from a storm? Of course not. That mountain is immovable.

I'll be honest with you. My own faith has not always been unshakable. When I was in college, I had a professor in a religion class who poked holes in the Bible and what it said. He brought up questions I had never asked myself about what I believed. Those questions started me on a chaotic journey that ended with me walking away from my faith for a time. I was lost and confused. I wasn't a mountain of immovability. I was a desert in the midst of a sandstorm, blowing all over the place. For a time, I explored other religions. My hope in God had disappeared, and I faced the reality of life without hope. Spoiler alert: it's a terrible place to be.

Those years of searching are ones that I often think back on. I still struggle with doubts. Every Christian will. I still have questions that I've never found answers to. But my trust muscles are so much stronger now. I've made my faith into a mountain that is rooted in the Word of God, and what He says is true. So when the earthquakes come, I'm unshakable. There will be earthquakes, my friend. How is your foundation?

God, I want to have unshakable faith
that will stand up to the shakings of doubt.
I do trust in You. I trust in Your Word and who You are.
Help me to stay strong and unshakable in my faith. Amen.

Love God. Love People. Tell Others.

Jesus replied, "'You must love the LORD your God with all your heart, all your soul, and all your mind.' This is the first and greatest commandment. A second is equally important: 'Love your neighbor as yourself.' The entire law and all the demands of the prophets are based on these two commandments."

MATTHEW 22:37–40 NLT

What greater mission statement than: Love God. Love People. Tell Others. Jesus lays it out pretty clearly in Matthew 22:37 and 39. He says, "You must love the LORD your God with all your heart, all your soul, and all your mind" and "Love your neighbor as yourself." Those two commands may seem childish, but they are absolutely profound. If the entire world simply lived by those six words—Love God. Love People. Tell Others—there would be true peace. It's our job to bring God's peace everywhere we go when we live by this motto. It will change your life if you filter your experiences through this simple lens.

Do you love God with all your heart, soul, mind, and strength? Do you truly, authentically love the people who God puts in your path? Do you talk to your friends and family about what God has done in your heart? Living on mission doesn't necessarily mean that you move overseas as a missionary. It can start right now, today, by simply living out the mission that Jesus gave to us. It's a simple message, but the truth of those six simple words could change everything for you.

God, I do love You with all that I am.
I am so grateful that You have saved me from my own destruction. Show me how to love people like You do. Amen.

YOUR MOVE:
Take some time to think about your own mission statement. What do you feel like God is putting on your heart as a life motto?

Regulating Emotions

And "don't sin by letting anger control you."
Don't let the sun go down while you are still angry,
for anger gives a foothold to the devil.

EPHESIANS 4:26–27 NLT

Anger is a feeling we all experience; it's completely natural. Whether it's a disagreement with a friend, frustration over schoolwork, or even feeling left out, those emotions can bubble up fast.

The feeling of anger isn't the problem; it's what we do with that anger that counts. The key is to manage our anger in a way that doesn't lead us to hurt others or make poor choices. Have you ever let anger take over and ended up saying something you regretted? I know I have! It's easy to let emotions run wild, but the better, more courageous option is to take a step back, breathe, and think before we act.

Before responding in anger, ask yourself these questions:

1. **What is causing me to feel this way?** Was this emotion caused by an event or my environment? Or did this emotion just pop up out of the blue?

2. **Could this be stemming from something deeper?** Dig a little into yourself to determine if there's a root to the emotion. Instead of instantly reacting in anger, think about your day. Was there something else that actually upset you?

3. **Am I projecting this emotion outward onto my family?** When you just want to explode at your family and release all that pent-up anger, *stop*. Those closest to us are often the ones that we hurt the most.

Next time you feel anger taking over your actions, try going on a walk, taking a shower, or sitting out on the porch. Pray. Think. Work through your feelings. Do what you need to do to take a calm step back into life to address the issue at hand and make it right.

Dear God, thank You for understanding our emotions. Help us to navigate our anger in a way that honors You and those around us. Amen.

House upon the Rock

"He is like a man building a house, who dug deep and laid the foundation on the rock. When the flood came, the river crashed against that house and couldn't shake it, because it was well built."

LUKE 6:48 CSB

There was a little kids' song that we used to sing in church on Sunday: "The wise man built his house upon the rock, the wise man built his house upon the rock, the wise man built his house upon the rock, and the rains came tumbling down." Trust me. If you learned that song as a child, it will stay with you for your entire life. What might seem like a silly kids' song is actually a really deep teaching from Jesus.

Jesus was teaching a big crowd. He told them, "I will show you what someone is like who comes to Me, hears My words, and acts on them: He is like a man building a house, who dug deep and laid the foundation on the rock. When the flood came, the river crashed against that house and couldn't shake it, because it was well built. But the one who hears and does not act is like a man who built a house on the ground without a foundation. The river crashed against it, and immediately it collapsed. And the destruction of that house was great" (Luke 6:47–49 CSB). What's the true difference between the two symbolic men? Is it their listening abilities? No. They both heard the words that Jesus said. Is it their house-making abilities? No. They both built a decent house.

It was their *obedience* that separates them. The man who heard Jesus's words and acted on them built his house on the rock. The man who heard Jesus's words and didn't act built his house on the sand, leaving his home open to the floods of life. Jesus often spoke in stories that had big truths hidden inside. Listening to sermons and occasionally reading the Bible is not acting on your faith. It's sloppy workmanship. We have to listen to what Jesus is saying and then do something about it. That obedience will build us up to be strong for those waves of the world that come to sweep us away. Which one are you? The wise house builder? Or the foolish one?

God, the easiest path is the one where I don't have to act,
but that way only leads to shaky foundations.
I want to do what You want me to do. Period.
Help me build my life on Your firm foundation. Amen.

Peace That Sticks

"I have told you all this so that you may have peace in Me. Here on earth you will have many trials and sorrows. But take heart, because I have overcome the world."

JOHN 16:33 NLT

We are all seeking something, even if we don't realize it. Peace. Hope. A purpose. When the world feels crazy, we want to feel a sense of safety and comfort. But can we truly have peace in this life?

Yes. We. Can. Jesus tells us, "I have told you all this so that you may have peace in Me. Here on earth you will have many trials and sorrows. But take heart, because I have overcome the world" (John 16:33). Jesus had a purpose when He walked the earth: to bring true peace to mankind. Peace is not simply the absence of conflict. It's a state of living, and it's only truly discovered when we give control to God. Peace is not impacted by circumstance. It's immovable. When we fully embrace the peace that Jesus offers, it cannot be stolen away. Peace found in God will keep us strong and calm when bad things happen and when the world feels like it's falling apart.

Remember the last part of that verse. Jesus has overcome the world, so we can be brave. We can trust that God is in control. He has a plan for all of this, and we can trust Him. None of us wants peace that only lasts for a day. We all want a peace that lasts a lifetime. A peace that sticks. We don't want the glue sticks that we used in kindergarten that barely held two pages of construction paper together. We want the heavy-duty glue that is so strong you don't even want to touch it or get it on your skin. That's the kind of sticky peace we want. And that kind of peace comes when we embed ourselves in the Bible and learn from Jesus. It's easier to feel at peace when we're walking right next to Jesus through the storm.

Jesus, I want that peace that sticks.
I'm tired of feeling out of control.
I want to learn to trust You despite the circumstances.
You're in control of it all. Amen.

Chosen

But you are not like that, for you are a chosen people.
You are royal priests, a holy nation, God's very own possession.
As a result, you can show others the goodness of God,
for He called you out of the darkness into His wonderful light.

I PETER 2:9 NLT

Your generation has an immense amount of passion and love to offer the world. You can be a world-changer. You're incredibly special. The fact that you've invested your time and energy into reading through this devotional book speaks to your desire to learn and grow. God loves that you want to know Him. He's eager to show Himself to you. And this has been a great journey of getting to know Him more and learning to trust Him with our tomorrows . . . to embrace the resilient hope that He offers to us.

You were created for this moment in history. Chosen for a purpose. Crafted with care. God placed you in your family, in your town, in your friend group . . . for a reason. He has a great plan for your life. Wherever life takes you, however far you travel, whether or not you stray from your faith . . . God will never, ever give up on you. He loves you so completely, so perfectly. And He simply wants to have a relationship with you all the days of your life.

Your life matters. What you do matters. How you live matters. We each will leave a mark on the world that remains long after we're gone. It's our job to decide what mark we'll leave. Live each day to the fullest. Love people with the same love that God shows you. Read His Word, the Bible. And walk in lockstep with Jesus. If you do those things, you're setting yourself up for a life of purpose, of faith, and of resilient hope.

God, thank You for choosing me.
Thank You for loving me, no matter what I do.
No one deserves the love that You offer,
but You offer it anyway. Thank You. Amen.

YOUR MOVE:
Life change is made to be shared! If you loved this devotional, share it with a friend and tell her what you learned.

Dear Friend,

This book was prayerfully crafted with you, the reader, in mind. Every word, every sentence, every page was thoughtfully written, designed, and packaged to encourage you—right where you are this very moment. At DaySpring, our vision is to see every person experience the life-changing message of God's love. So, as we worked through rough drafts, design changes, edits, and details, we prayed for you to deeply experience His unfailing love, indescribable peace, and pure joy. It is our sincere hope that through these Truth-filled pages your heart will be blessed, knowing that God cares about you—your desires and disappointments, your challenges and dreams.

He knows. He cares. He loves you unconditionally.

BLESSINGS!
THE DAYSPRING BOOK TEAM